Youth Edi

In God's Presence

Your Daily Guide to a Meaningful Prayer Life

T. W. HUNT & CLAUDE V. KING

LifeWay Press
Nashville, Tennessee

7200-64
ISBN 0-7673-0001-7

Dewey Decimal Classification: 248.32
Subject Heading: Prayer/SPIRITUAL LIFE

This book is the text for course CG-0249 in the subject area Prayer in
the Christian Growth Study Plan.

Unless otherwise indicated, Scripture quotations are from the Holy
Bible, *New International Version,* copyright © 1973, 1978, 1984 by
International Bible Society

Art Direction: Edward Crawford
Cover Illustration: Nicolas Wilton

Printed in the United States of America
Available from Baptist Book Stores

Produced by the Youth Section
Discipleship and Family Development Division
of The Sunday School Board
of the Southern Baptist Convention
127 Ninth Avenue, North, Nashville, Tennessee 37234

CONTENTS

THE AUTHORS

T. W. Hunt has given much of his life to teaching others the ways of the Lord. For 24 years he taught music and missions at Southwestern Baptist Theological Seminary in Fort Worth, Texas. For 7 years prior to his retirement T.W. served as a prayer consultant for the Sunday School Board of the Southern Baptist Convention. He was a member of the Bold Mission Prayer Thrust Team that issued a Call to Prayer and Solemn Assembly on September 17, 1989.

T. W. is a graduate of Ouachita Baptist College and holds Master of Music and Doctor of Philosophy degrees from North Texas State University. In addition to numerous articles, T. W. has written several books, including *Music in Missions: Discipling Through Music, The Doctrine of Prayer, Disciple's Prayer Life: Walking in Fellowship with God* (with Catherine Walker), and *The Mind of Christ*. T. W. also compiled and wrote portions of the Church Prayer Ministry Manual.

T. W. is married to his childhood sweetheart, Laverne. They have one daughter, Melana, and five grandchildren. T. W. and Laverne make their home in Spring, Texas.

Claude V. King is Mission Service Corps Consultant, Office of Prayer and Spiritual Awakening, Home Mission Board of the Southern Baptist Convention. He is active in discipleship training and is becoming recognized as a writer of interactive learning activities. Claude coauthored another LIFE course with John Drakeford entitled *WiseCounsel: Skills for Lay Counseling*. He has served as a volunteer church planter for the Concord Baptist Association of middle Tennessee.

A native of Tennessee, he is a graduate of Belmont University and New Orleans Baptist Theological Seminary. He lives in Murfreesboro, Tennessee, with his wife, Reta, and daughters, Julie and Jenny.

INTRODUCTION

Purposes of This Study

Prayer is not a religious ritual for Christians to practice one, two, or three times a day. Prayer is a relationship God has with His children. It is an intimate and personal relationship. Prayer is a time for you to enter the presence of your Heavenly Father, the Creator and Ruler of the universe. Prayer is a holy privilege.

We have prepared this course for two purposes:
1. To help you develop a meaningful, well-balanced, and daily prayer life. You will understand and use six kinds of prayer in your daily prayer life.
2. To help you pray effectively with other believers. God has made a special promise about praying together: *"If two of you on earth agree about anything you ask for, it will be done for you by my Father in heaven. For where two or three come together in my name, there am I with them" (Matt. 18:19-20).* God promises great authority to prayers of agreement among believers. God also promises a greater dimension of His presence when two or three meet to pray. We want you to experience the joy, power, and intimacy that united prayer brings. Praying together, however, is not just adding together several individual prayers in sequence. Praying together effectively is a conversation among believers and God. Learning to pray together will be a most rewarding adventure.

Studying This Course

This six-week study consists of two important components:
1. Individual study. You will study individual lessons five days each week. Study only one lesson each day and use what you are learning in your daily prayer life. Each lesson should take from 10 to 15 minutes. You may choose, however, to spend more time in personal prayer. Do not omit the learning activities. They are designed to help you learn and apply what you study. They should help enrich your personal prayer experiences.
2. Small-group prayer. You will join one or more other believers in a weekly prayer group. The time you spend together will not be a time to talk about prayer. It will be a time to pray. Your small group could consist of you and your family, friends, members of your youth group at church, fellow participants in a prayer ministry, class, or ongoing study group. You could even use this study to revitalize a midweek prayer service at church. Scan the list below and check one or more possible groups with which you could begin praying together.

☐ Family members
☐ Friends at church
☐ Friends at school
☐ Friends in your community
☐ Group of teachers at church
☐ Interdenominational prayer group
☐ Midweek prayer service
☐ Missions group
☐ Multiethnic group
☐ Prayer group
☐ Prayer-ministry participants
☐ Prayer partner(s)
☐ Other

Whatever location or group you choose, keep the size of your prayer group small—not more than eight persons. This will allow everyone to participate actively in praying. If you use this study for a large group, divide the large group into smaller groups for more intimate praying.

Leadership

Select a leader for your group prayer time, enlisting either the same person for the entire study or a different person each week. The leader may be an adult or a respected member of your youth group. The leader may be you. No guide for the leader is provided since the small-group experience is a prayer time. However, suggestions for prayer sessions are provided on page 93. The leader may lead the prayer time by following the suggestions in the guide but should feel free to adapt the suggestions to meet the prayer needs of your group. By the end of your study, your group may be so experienced praying together that the Holy Spirit will be the only guide you will need!

A Prayer Project

Charles Haddon Spurgeon, a well-known 19th-century preacher in London, attributed much of the power in his preaching to a group of men who met in the boiler room of the church to pray while he was preaching. You may want to consider participating in a similar prayer project during or after this study. Adults in your church may have already begun a prayer ministry. If so, join them. Offer to take some of the responsibility. It may even become an ongoing part of your church's intercessory prayer ministry.

1. Set aside a prayer room and enlist several persons to pray together during worship services. Intercessors may rotate from week to week so that they may also attend services. Tell your pastor about your desire to have a prayer room in your church. He will be positive and encouraging.
2. Provide copies of a prayer-request card for persons attending worship services. A model, called "Prayer Requests," is provided on page 7, which you have permission to duplicate or adapt. Ask your pastor if you can print the card as a part of your order of worship or print it on card stock to place in pew racks. Before the service begins, invite persons to submit prayer requests. Collect the cards early in the service and deliver them to the prayer room.
3. Persons in the prayer room should divide into groups of two or three and divide the prayer-request cards among the groups. Each group should pray for the specific needs indicated on their cards, as well as for the pastor and other participants in the worship service. Persons submit prayer-request cards in faith. Intercessors can join in faith to offer these requests to God as these persons worship.
4. When God answers prayers, be sure to give Him the credit. Give persons opportunities to testify to the ways God has answered their requests.
5. Encourage the intercessors by showing them ways they are laboring with God in His work. The call to intercession is a high calling. Both Jesus and the Holy Spirit are intercessors. Those who are called to be intercessors become laborers with God in mighty kingdom work.

PRAYER REQUESTS

During our worship service today Christians in our prayer room are praying for you and this service. These persons are trained and prepared to pray for you and your family about spiritual decisions, as well as other needs you may have today. If you would permit them to pray for your request, please fill out this prayer-request card. You do not have to give your name. If you choose to give your name, specific requests will be held in strict confidence.

Your name (optional):

_____

Age group (circle one):

Adult   Youth   Child

Please pray during this service that God will work in my life in the following areas:
❑ I need to become a Christian.
❑ I am no longer close to God, and I need to return to an intimate fellowship with Him.
❑ I am seeking God's direction about a church home in this community.
❑ I am lonely and need Christian fellowship.
❑ I have sinned and need to confess, repent, and experience God's cleansing and forgiveness.
❑ My spouse/child is not a Christian. Name (optional):

_____

❑ My spouse/child is a Christian but is not close to the Lord. Name (optional):

_____

❑ My child is living in rebellion. Pray that he/she will return to the Lord. Name (optional):

_____

❑ I am experiencing problems in my marriage, and I need God's help with our reconciliation.

❑ I think God may be calling me to a church vocation or to missions.
❑ I have an important decision to make, and I want to know God's will.
❑ I am facing a moral decision, and I need strength to obey God.
❑ I am hurting because of:

_____

_____

❑ Someone in this service needs to make a spiritual decision. Name (optional):

_____

❑ Other request(s):

_____

_____

_____

_____

❑ Please also share my request(s) with the pastor.

During the worship service instructions will be given for the collection of prayer-request cards.

Week 1
Six Kinds of Prayer

This Weeks Scripture-Memory Verse

"If you remain in me and my words remain in you, ask whatever you wish, and it will be given you" (John 15:7).

This Weeks Lessons

Day 1: Prayer Is a Relationship
Day 2: Responding and Asking Prayers
Day 3: Four Kinds of Responding Prayers
Day 4: Two Kinds of Asking Prayers
Day 5: Praying with Others

Summary of Week 1

This week you will:

- overview this six-week study;
- understand that the nature of prayer is an intimate love relationship with God;
- understand that God wants you to identify with Him by becoming like Him and by participating with Him in His work;
- understand and begin using the following six kinds of prayer in your daily prayer life.
  — Confession: responding to God's holiness
  — Praise: responding to God's attributes
  — Worship: responding to God's glory
  — Thanksgiving: responding to God's riches
  — Petition: asking that is led by your Heavenly Father
  — Intercession: asking that is led by your Master

This Weeks Prayer Focus: Confession

When you enter God's presence, you become aware of His holiness. In the presence of God's holiness you become aware of your sinfulness. Sin hinders your prayer relationship with God. *Confession* means *agreeing with God.* Confession includes agreeing with God about the nature of your sin, after which you seek God's cleansing and restoration to intimate fellowship. Confession is a good beginning place for prayer, preparing you to enter the presence of holy God.

Confession is also agreeing with God about the truth. You can confess who God is. You can agree with Him about who you are in relationship to Him. You can agree with Him about the truth of your circumstances or your need.

This week focus on the following Scriptures about confession. Let God prepare you to enter His presence!

Examples of Confession of Sin

David . . . said to the Lord, *"I have sinned greatly in what I have done. Now, O Lord, I beg you, take away the guilt of your servant. I have done a very foolish thing"* (2 Sam. 24:10).

"Our sins are higher than our heads and our guilt has reached to the heavens. From the days of our forefathers until now, our guilt has been great.
"But now, O our God, what can we say after this? For we have disregarded the commands you gave.
"O Lord, God of Israel, you are righteous!
. . . Here we are before you in our guilt, though because of it not one of us can stand in your presence" (Ezra 9:6-7,10-11,15).

Have mercy on me, O God,
according to your unfailing love;
according to your great compassion
blot out my transgressions.
Wash away all my iniquity
and cleanse me from my sin.
For I know my transgressions,

and my sin is always before me.
Against you, you only, have I sinned
    and done what is evil in your sight,
so that you are proved right when you speak
    and justified when you judge.
Cleanse me with hyssop, and I will be clean;
    wash me, and I will be whiter than snow.
Let me hear joy and gladness;
    let the bones you have crushed rejoice.
Hide your face from my sins
    and blot out all my iniquity.
Create in me a pure heart, O God,
    and renew a steadfast spirit within me.
Do not cast me from your presence
    or take your Holy Spirit from me.
Restore to me the joy of your salvation
    and grant me a willing spirit,
        to sustain me.
Then I will teach transgressors your ways,
    and sinners will turn back to you
        (Ps. 51:1-4,7-13)

Although our sins testify against us,
    O Lord, do something for the sake of
        your name.
For our backsliding is great;
    we have sinned against you (Jer. 14:7).

" 'Forgive us our debts,
    as we also have forgiven our debtors' "
        (Matt. 6:12)

Group Confession

Those of Israelite descent . . . stood in their places and confessed their sins and the wickedness of their fathers. They stood where they were and read from the Book of the Law of the Lord their God for a quarter of the day, and spent another quarter in confession and in worshiping the Lord their God (Neh. 9:2-3).

Confession of Truth

Simon Peter answered, "You are the Christ, the Son of the living God" (Matt. 16:16).

"Sovereign Lord, . . . you made the heaven and the earth and the sea, and everything in them" (Acts 4:24).

Promise for Confession

If we confess our sins, he is faithful and just and will forgive us our sins and purify us from all unrighteousness (1 John 1:9).

Day 1
Prayer Is a Relationship

SCRIPTURE-MEMORY VERSE
"If you remain in me and my words remain in you, ask whatever you wish, and it will be given you" (John 15:7).

Prayer is not one-sided communication with a distant God. Prayer is a conversation between you and God, a relationship between you and your Creator. God desires your fellowship. More than anything else, He wants you to love Him with all your being. He also wants you to know and experience His love and presence. God is seeking that kind of relationship with you!

▶ Read *Revelation 3:20* and *John 14:23* below. Underline the words that describe the relationship God wants to have with you.

DEUTERONOMY 6:5
Love the Lord your God with all your heart and with all your soul and with all your strength.

"Here I am! I stand at the door and knock. If anyone hears my voice and opens the door, I will come in and eat with him, and he with me" (Rev. 3:20).

"If anyone loves me, he will obey my teaching. My Father will love him, and we will come to him and make our home with him" (John 14:23).

God seeks a love relationship with you. He is knocking. Will you invite Him in? Will you enjoy fellowship with Him? Will you love Him? Will you permit Him to live with you? You may have already entered a saving relationship with Jesus Christ. For the remainder of this study, we will assume that you have done so. If you have not, find a pastor or a Christian friend to help you accept Christ as your Savior and Lord. This love relationship is the point at which effective prayer begins.

A love relationship with God is the point at which effective prayer begins.

▶ Pause and thank God for inviting you into a love relationship with Him. Ask Him to deepen your experience of His presence in prayer as you complete this course.

In *John 15:7*, this week's Scripture-memory verse, Jesus makes a special promise to those who abide in Him. If you have a love relationship with Him and His words (teachings and commands) have become a part of your life, Jesus promises to respond to your prayers. The need for His words to remain in you is an important reason you are encouraged to memorize a Scripture passage each week of this study.

Jesus promises to respond to your prayers.

What is the prayer promise Jesus made in *John 15:7?*
"Ask whatever you wish, and _____."

Begin memorizing *John 15:7*. Read it several times. Repeat it aloud phrase by phrase until you can say it without looking. Review it each week of your study.

Jesus also makes a special prayer promise to those who pray together in His name: *"If two of you on earth agree about anything you ask for, it will be done for you by my Father in heaven. For where two or three come together in my name, there am I with them" (Matt. 18:19-20).* In this passage Jesus makes two promises for united prayer in which two or more pray together in agreement:
1. God gives greater authority to united prayer.
2. God is present where two or more gather in His name.
This course was also designed to help you experience these two promises. We want you to learn the great authority God has granted to believers when they pray together in agreement. Many people are not seeing answers to prayer. This says more about their praying than it does about God. He has not changed. He still answers prayer. We will help you learn to pray more effectively as you follow biblical patterns for prayer.

This course was also designed to help you pray with other believers. God promises that those who gather to pray in His name experience a greater dimension of His presence.

Those who gather to pray in His name experience a greater dimension of His presence.

Have you made plans to pray with other believers as you study this course? ❏ Yes ❏ No

With whom will you be praying?

_____

If you have not made plans, begin to do so now. See pages 5-6 for suggestions.

Each day you will close your study with a prayer time. Today talk to the Lord about your love relationship with Him. Share with Him your desires for this study.

Day 2
Responding and Asking Prayers

TODAY'S PRAYER PROMISE
" 'Call to me and I will answer you and tell you great and unsearchable things you do not know' " (Jer. 33:3).

God takes the initiative in prayer. It does not begin with you. He begins the relationship. God comes to you and gives you the desire to spend time with Him in prayer. It is God who works in you to will and to act according to His good purpose *(Phil. 2:13)*.

▶ Where does prayer begin?
- ❏ Prayer begins with me. I am the one who chooses to pray.
- ❏ Prayer begins with God. He causes me to want to pray.

Prayer always begins with God. Even though you may think you decide to pray, God is the One who gives you the desire. Whenever you have the desire to pray, God is extending a personal invitation for you to spend time with Him. In prayer God wants you to identify with Him in two ways:

PURPOSES IN PRAYER
1. **To identify with God by becoming like Him.**
2. **To identify with God by working with Him in prayer.**

1. God wants you to identify with Him by becoming like His perfect Son, Jesus Christ.
2. God also wants you to identify with His purposes. He wants you to cooperate in accomplishing His purposes by asking for things that will advance His kingdom (His rule). You identify with Him by working with Him in prayer.

God gave you different kinds of prayer to accomplish these two patterns of identification with Him. During our study we will learn about six kinds of prayer, which fall into two groups. Some prayer is responding to God. In responding prayers you respond to God as a Person. You are learning to be a certain kind of person—a person like God Himself. Being is the important emphasis. As you talk to Him, God leads you to know Him and His ways so that you can become like Him.

▶ What is one group of prayers?

R_____ prayers

RESPONDING PRAYERS
Confession
Praise
Worship
Thanksgiving

Responding prayers include confession, praise, worship, and thanksgiving. These are listed for you in the chart on page 95.

The other group of prayers is *asking prayers.* In asking prayers you are concerned with God's work. *Doing* is the important emphasis. As God leads your asking, you become involved with Him in His work.

⮔ **What is another group of prayers?**

A _____ prayers

Asking prayers include prayers of petition, in which you pray for yourself and God's work in your life. Asking prayers also include intercession, in which you pray for God's work in and through others.

ASKING PRAYERS
Petition
Intercession

⮔ **Drawing lines across the columns, match the groups of prayer on the left with the purposes of identification with God on the right.**

Responding prayers   Participating in God's work
Asking prayers   Becoming like God

In responding prayers you identify with God by becoming like Him. For instance, God reveals His holiness to you by revealing His purity. Then you may see impurities in your life. You respond to God's holiness by confessing and turning away from your impurities. Through this responding prayer you become more like God.

In responding prayers you identify with God by becoming like Him.

⮔ **Using the chart on page 95, write below the four kinds of responding prayers.**

C _____ is responding to God's holiness.

P _____ is responding to God's attributes.

W _____ is responding to God's glory.

T _____ is responding to God's riches.

In asking prayers you identify with God by participating with Him in His work. For instance, God as your Master may lead you to ask Him for friends to join you in starting a Christian club in your school. God answers your prayer by giving a fellow classmate the desire to be a part of a Christian club. When they respond, you know that God accomplished His purposes in answer to prayer. Through this asking prayer you worked together with God.

In asking prayers you identify with God by participating with Him in His work.

⮔ **Using the chart on page 95, write the two kinds of asking prayers.**

P _____ is asking that is led by your Heavenly Father.

I _____ is asking that is led by your Master.

Pray, asking God to help you become more like Him. Agree to allow God to involve you in His work.

Day 3
Four Kinds of Responding Prayers

TODAY'S PRAYER PROMISE
"Sacrifice thank offerings to God, fulfill your vows to the Most High, and call upon me in the day of trouble; I will deliver you, and you will honor me" (Ps. 50:14-15).

God wants you, as His child, to identify with Him by becoming like Him. God reveals Himself and His ways to you so that you can become like Him. In a love relationship with you, God reveals what He is like. As you respond to Him in that relationship, you can become more like Him. We have identified four kinds of responding prayers:

1. Confession   3. Worship
2. Praise   4. Thanksgiving

▶ Which of the following is the purpose of responding prayers?
   ❑ I identify with God by working with Him in His Kingdom.
   ❑ I identify with God by becoming like Him.

By responding to God in prayer, you become more like Him.

CONFESSION
Have mercy on me, O God, according to your unfailing love; according to your great compassion blot out my transgressions. Wash away all my iniquity and cleanse me from my sin. For I know my transgressions, and my sin is always before me. Against you, you only, have I sinned and done what is evil in your sight, so that you are proved right when you speak and justified when

Confession: Responding to God's Holiness

One trait God reveals about Himself is that He is holy. He is separate, pure, and righteous. God reveals that He is holy and that He wants you to be holy like Him. He wants you to be pure and set apart for His purposes.

But sometimes you are not holy. You sin. Because sin is offensive to God, it hinders your intimate fellowship with Him. The Holy Spirit convicts you of the sin, and you can use a prayer of confession to restore the fellowship. Confession is saying the same thing God says, or agreeing with God. You agree with God about the nature of your sin. Because you love Him, you want to return to Him (repent) and become more like Him. Confession is responding to God's holiness.

▶ What is one kind of responding prayer?

   C_____

Confession is responding to what aspect of God?

H_____

Read in the margin an example of confession.

Praise: Responding to God's Attributes

God reveals His attributes or character traits because He wants you to become like Him. As you grow in your knowledge of God, you will know His attributes. When you know what God is like, you want to praise Him. Praise lifts up or focuses on God's attributes. Praise exalts God in His divinity—because of what He is like. Praise is responding to God's attributes.

▶ What is a second kind of responding prayer?

P_____

Praise is responding to what aspects of God?

A_____

Read in the margin an example of praise.

Worship: Responding to God's Glory

When God acts to reveal Himself, He displays His glory. Glory is the evidence of God's attributes (what He is like). God reveals His glory through His mighty acts. All creation reveals God's glory. When you see God's glory, you love Him. Worship is responding to God's glory.

Worship is adoring, loving, and honoring God. Worship is much more personal and intimate than praise. Worship is the expression of your love, adoration, reverence, and honor for God.

▶ What is a third kind of responding prayer?

W_____

Worship is responding to what aspect of God?

G_____

Read in the margin an example of worship.

you judge. . . . Create in me a pure heart, O God, and renew a steadfast spirit within me. . . . Restore to me the joy of your salvation and grant me a willing spirit, to sustain me (Ps. 51:1-4,10,12).

PRAISE
Great is the Lord and most worthy of praise; his greatness no one can fathom. One generation will commend your works to another; they will tell of your mighty acts. They will speak of the glorious splendor of your majesty, and I will meditate on your wonderful works. They will tell of the power of your awesome works, and I will proclaim your great deeds. They will celebrate your abundant goodness and joyfully sing of your righteousness (Ps. 145:3-7).

WORSHIP
As the deer pants for streams of water, so my soul pants for you, O God. My soul thirsts for God, for the living God (Ps. 42:1-2).

THANKSGIVING

Give thanks to the Lord, for he is good. His love endures forever . . . who spread out the earth upon the waters, . . . to the One who remembered us in our low estate . . . and freed us from our enemies. . . . Give thanks to the God of heaven. His love endures forever (Ps. 136:1,6,23-24,26).

Thanksgiving: Responding to God's Riches

God reveals His riches—both physical and spiritual. God is the Giver of every perfect gift. He wants you to experience the abundant life He has to give you. Thanksgiving is responding to and participating in God's riches.

Ephesians 5:20 tells you to thank God in everything. Thanksgiving is not just an event or a statement. It is an attitude. God wants you to have an attitude of gratitude.

What is a fourth kind of responding prayer?

T _____

Thanksgiving is responding to what aspect of God?

R _____

Read in the margin an example of thanksgiving.

Review the four kinds of responding prayers. Then spend a few minutes praying and responding to evidences of God's holiness, attributes, glory, and riches.

Day 4
Two Kinds of Asking Prayers

TODAY'S PRAYER PROMISE
This is the confidence we have in approaching God: that if we ask anything according to his will, he hears us. And if we know that he hears us—whatever we ask—we know that we have what we asked of him (1 John 5:14-15).

In responding prayers you respond to the person of God or to the aspects of who He is (holiness, attributes, glory, riches). The other group of prayers is asking prayers, emphasized in Jesus' greatest teaching sessions.

"Ask and it will be given to you; seek and you will find; knock and the door will be opened to you" (Matt. 7:7).

"You may ask me for anything in my name, and I will do it" (John 14:14).

"If you remain in me and my words remain in you, ask whatever you wish, and it will be given you" (John 15:7).

"Until now you have not asked for anything in my name. Ask and you will receive, and your joy will be complete" (John 16:24).

▶ To review yesterday's lesson, list the four kinds of responding prayers. Check your answers on page 95.

C _____ is responding to God's holiness.

P _____ is responding to God's attributes.

W _____ is responding to God's glory.

T _____ is responding to God's riches.

The Bible teaches two kinds of asking prayers: petition and intercession. Asking prayers are not direct responses to the Person of God. As God takes the lead in the asking prayers, you follow His leading and participate with Him in His work. The great purpose in asking prayers is for you to identify with God's purposes. God is interested in your asking prayers. God wants you to cooperate in accomplishing His purposes by asking for things that will advance His kingdom (His rule).

▶ Which of the following is the purpose of asking prayers?
  ❑ I identify with God by working with Him in His Kingdom.
  ❑ I identify with God by becoming like Him.

Through asking prayers God brings about His purposes in your life and in the lives of others for whom you pray by involving you in His work. Let's overview the two kinds of asking prayers.

Petition: Asking That Is Led by Your Heavenly Father

Petition is asking for yourself, your family, your church, or your group. God reveals Himself as a Father. When you are redeemed, you are adopted into His family. As His child, you address your requests to your Heavenly Father.

God's purpose in encouraging your petition is to mold you into a certain kind of person—someone who is already in the mind of God. Because your personal petition should be directed by your Heavenly Father, through this kind of prayer you become more like the person God wants you to be as He accomplishes His purposes in your life.

Read in the margin two examples of petition.

INDIVIDUAL PETITION
(David's prayer for himself)
To you, O Lord, I lift up my soul; in you I trust, O my God. Do not let me be put to shame, nor let my enemies triumph over me. . . . Show me your ways, O Lord, teach me your paths; guide me in your truth and teach me, for you are God my Savior, and my hope is in you all day long (Ps. 25:1-2,4-5).

GROUP PETITION
(The early church's prayer for itself)
"Sovereign Lord," . . . "you made the heaven and the earth and the sea, and everything in them. Now, Lord, consider their threats and enable your servants to speak your word with great boldness. Stretch out your hand to heal and perform miraculous signs and wonders through the name of your holy servant Jesus" (Acts 4:24,29-30).

▶ What is one kind of asking prayer?

P_____

Who leads your petitions? _____

INTERCESSION

(Paul's prayer for the Ephesians)
I pray that out of his glorious riches he may strengthen you with power through his Spirit in your inner being, so that Christ may dwell in your hearts through faith. And I pray that you, being rooted and established in love, may have power, together with all the saints, to grasp how wide and long and high and deep is the love of Christ, and to know this love that surpasses knowledge—that you may be filled to the measure of all the fullness of God (Eph. 3:16-19).

Intercession: Asking That Is Led by Your Master

God reveals Himself as Master and Ruler. God is at work in His world, and He has chosen to do His work through people. When God gets ready to do something, He calls a person to intercession, which is asking for someone else. Your Master leads your intercession for others. Through intercession you work with God as His servant. Intercession is an important method God uses to accomplish His will among people.

▶ What is the second kind of asking prayer

I_____

Who leads your intercession?_____

Read in the margin the example of intercession. Underline the requests made of God in behalf of others.

Pause to pray, using Paul's requests in Ephesians 3:16-19. First pray these requests for yourself. Then pray these requests for your church or prayer group.

Day 5
Praying with Others

We hope you have been paying attention to the prayer promise at the beginning of each day. You may want to write the most meaningful ones on index cards and memorize them.

TODAY'S PRAYER PROMISE

This is what the high and lofty One says—he who lives forever, whose name is holy: "I live in a high and holy place, but also with him who is contrite and lowly in spirit, to revive the spirit of the

▶ Read today's prayer promise. What are some of the ways God is described in this verse?

_____

_____

What are two places in which He chooses to dwell?

_____

_____

What are two reasons He chooses to dwell with those who are humble and contrite?

_____

_____

> *lowly and to revive the heart of the contrite" (Isa. 57:15).*

▶ Which pair of the following characteristics best describes you?
   ❑ Humble and contrite
   ❑ Proud, arrogant, remorseless

If you are interested in praying in God's presence, you need to develop the character of one with whom God dwells. He brings the humble and contrite into His presence. He does not dwell with the proud and arrogant.

Day 5 of each week in this study focuses on praying together. Often, we are so familiar with praying alone that we pray with others the same way we do by ourselves. Does the following describe prayer meetings you have attended?

1. The first person prays through his mental list while other group members check off these subjects on their mental lists.
2. The second person prays through the remaining items on her mental list while other group members check off items on their mental lists.
3. The next person has little left on his list about which to pray.
4. The last person feeling that almost everything has been covered, closes the prayer time.

Not every group prayer time is like that. However, we miss some exciting dimensions of praying together if we only pray through mental lists. We suggest that you and your prayer group consider some guidelines for praying together more effectively.

> **To pray in God's presence, develop the character of one with whom God dwells.**

▶ Read "Suggestions for Praying Together" on page 93. In each suggestion underline a word or a phrase to help you remember it.

Now review the words or phrases. Circle the numbers beside the three suggestions that will be most helpful for your prayer group to practice.

MATTHEW 18:20
"Where two or three come together in my name, there am I with them."

ROMANS 8:26-27,34
The Spirit helps us in our weakness. We do not know what we ought to pray for, but the Spirit himself intercedes for us with groans that words cannot express. And he who searches our hearts knows the mind of the Spirit, because the Spirit intercedes for the saints in accordance with God's will. Christ Jesus, who died—more than that, who was raised to life—is at the right hand of God and is also interceding for us.

HEBREWS 7:25
He [Christ] is able to save completely those who come to God through him, because he always lives to intercede for them.

1 JOHN 1:9
"If we confess our sins, he is faithful and just and will forgive us our sins and purify us from all unrighteousness."

At least once each week we will discuss ways your prayer group can pray together more effectively. Today we will examine two suggestions.

Acknowledge God's Presence and Active Participation

God has promised His presence where two or more are gathered in His name (see *Matt. 18:20*). He is also actively involved when you pray together. Both the Holy Spirit and Jesus intercede for and with you (see *Rom. 8:26-27,34; Heb. 7:25*). When you meet with a group to pray, remember that God is present. Think of your prayer time as a conversation among your group members and God. Speak to God. Listen to what God may say to you. And you may speak to one another as well as share prayer concerns during your prayer.

> When your group gathers to pray this week, who should be the focus of attention?
> ❑ I should be the focus of attention. I am important.
> ❑ Our group leader should be the focus. We need her guidance.
> ❑ God must be the focus. He is the most important One present.

Because prayer is a conversation among your group members and God, He should be the focus of your time together.

Prepare Yourselves Through Prayers of Confession, Cleansing, and Reconciliation

If you were entering the court of a king or a queen, you would want to be prepared. You would want to dress and act correctly. In a similar way, your group will want to prepare for entering the throne room of heaven. Jesus has made a way for your cleansing as you confess and turn from your sin (see *1 John 1:9*). In your prayer-group meeting take time for individuals to prepare themselves. Allow time for confession that members may need.

Using this week's introductory material on confession (pp. 8-9), spend time in prayers of confession. Ask God to cleanse you thoroughly. Pray for your prayer-group members as they also prepare for your time together in prayer this week.

Week 2
Developing Your Prayer Life

This Week's Scripture-Memory Verse
"If two of you on earth agree about anything you ask for, it will be done for you by my Father in heaven" (Matt.. 18:19).

This Week's Lessons
Day 1: Reasons to Pray
Day 2: Daily Prayer
Day 3: Tools to Help You Pray
Day 4: The Bible and Prayer
Day 5: Being a House of Prayer

Summary of Week 2
When you are related to your Heavenly Father by adoption, prayer is a natural part of the relationship. You talk to Him, and He talks to you. This relationship can be neglected or developed. This week we want to help you develop your personal prayer relationship with your Heavenly Father. This week you will:

- identify 10 reasons to pray;
- learn how prayer can and should be a constant, natural part of your day;
- use some practical tools to enrich your personal prayer life;
- learn ways to use the Bible in your prayers;
- understand the importance of your church's being a house of prayer.

This Week's Prayer Focus: Praise
In many different ways God reveals to you what He is like. His character traits are called His attributes. Praise is lifting up the attributes of God. You have a tendency to become like what you value or praise. By lifting up God's attributes in praise, you respond to Him by becoming more like Him. Through praise you elevate Him in the eyes and ears of others.

This week focus on the following Scriptures of praise. Respond to the Lord in prayer by lifting up His attributes. Allow Him to work freely in your life to mold you into the image of His perfect Son, Jesus Christ.

Examples of Praise

I will praise you, O Lord, with all my heart;
I will tell of all your wonders.
I will be glad and rejoice in you;
I will sing praise to your name,
O Most High (Ps. 9:1-2).

I will declare your name to my brothers;
in the congregation I will praise you
(Ps. 22:22).

Like your name, O God,
your praise reaches to the ends
of the earth;
your right hand is filled with righteousness
(Ps. 48:10).

I will praise you, O Lord, among the nations;
I will sing of you among the peoples.
For great is your love, reaching to the heavens;
your faithfulness reaches to the skies
(Ps. 57:9-10).

Because your love is better than life,
my lips will glorify you (Ps. 63:3).

You are my God, and I will give you thanks;
you are my God, and I will exalt you
(Ps. 118:28).

Seven times a day I praise you
    for your righteous laws (Ps. 119:164).

I will praise you, O Lord, with all my heart;
    before the "gods" I will sing your praise.
I will bow down toward your holy temple
    and will praise your name
    for your love and your faithfulness,
for you have exalted above all things
    your name and your word (Ps. 138:1-2).

I praise you because I am fearfully
    and wonderfully made;
    your works are wonderful,
    I know that full well (Ps. 139:14).

Great is the Lord and most worthy of praise;
    his greatness no one can fathom.
One generation will commend your works
    to another;
    they will tell of your mighty acts.
They will speak of the glorious splendor
    of your majesty,
    and I will meditate on your wonderful
    works (Ps. 145:3-5).

Mary's Praise

"My soul glorifies the Lord
    and my spirit rejoices in God my Savior,
    for the Mighty One has done great
    things for me—
    holy is his name.
His mercy extends to those who fear him,
    from generation to generation.
He has performed mighty deeds with
    his arm" (Luke 1:46-47,49-51).

Praise Commended

Praise the Lord.
    How good it is to sing praises to our God,
    how pleasant and fitting to praise him!
        (Ps. 147:1).

Praise the Lord.
    Praise God in his sanctuary;
    praise him in his mighty heavens.
Praise him for his acts of power;
    praise him for his surpassing greatness.
Praise him with the sounding of the trumpet,
    . . . with the harp and lyre,
. . . with tambourine and dancing,
    . . . with the strings and flute,
praise him with the clash of cymbals,
    . . . with resounding cymbals.
Let everything that has breath praise the Lord
        (Ps. 150).

"Give thanks to the Lord, call on his name;
    make known among the nations what
        he has done,
and proclaim that his name is exalted"
        (Isa. 12:4).

Through Jesus, therefore, let us continually
offer to God a sacrifice of praise—the fruit
of his lips that confess his name (Heb. 13:15).

Day 1
Reasons to Pray

Prayer is a relationship with your Heavenly Father. He created you for a love relationship with Himself. If you love someone, you want to spend time with him or her. If you love God, you want to spend time with Him. That conscious time you spend in God's presence is what we call prayer. One of the best reasons to pray is to spend time with the One you love.

▶ What is one of the best reasons to pray?

_____

Last week you studied two purposes in prayer. God wants you to identify with Him by becoming like Him. He also wants you to identify with Him by working together with Him.

▶ Read *John 15:16; Romans 8:29;* and *2 Corinthians 3:18* in the margin. Match the Scripture references below with the reasons to pray by drawing lines across the columns.

John 15:16   To become like God (Jesus)
Romans 8:29   To work together with God
2 Corinthians 3:18

John 15:16 focuses on prayer as working with God. The other two verses focus on becoming like Jesus.

▶ Read the following verses and identify other reasons to pray. Write a reason after each verse.

"Could you men not keep watch with me for one hour?" he asked Peter. "Watch and pray so that you will not fall into temptation" (Matt. 26:40-41).

_____

"The tax collector . . . beat his breast and said, 'God, have mercy on me, a sinner.'

SCRIPTURE-MEMORY VERSE
"If two of you on earth agree about anything you ask for, it will be done for you by my Father in heaven" (Matt. 18:19).

JOHN 15:16
"You did not choose me, but I chose you and appointed you to go and bear fruit—fruit that will last. Then the Father will give you whatever you ask in my name."

ROMANS 8:29
"Those God foreknew he also predestined to be conformed to the likeness of his Son."

2 CORINTHIANS 3:18
"We, who with unveiled faces all reflect the Lord's glory, are being transformed into his likeness with ever-increasing glory, which comes from the Lord, who is the Spirit."

"I tell you that this man . . . went home justified before God"
(Luke 18:13-14).

_____

"Ask and you will receive, and your joy will be complete" (John 16:24).

_____

We do not know what we ought to pray for, but the Spirit himself intercedes for us. . . . . in accordance with God's will (Rom. 8:26-27).

_____

Let us then approach the throne of grace with confidence, so that we may receive mercy and find grace to help us in our time of need (Heb. 4:16).

_____

Let us continually offer to God a sacrifice of praise (Heb. 13:15).

_____

You may have expressed them differently, but consider these reasons: to gain strength to resist temptation *(Matt. 26:40-41)*, to be justified (made right) with God *(Luke 18:13-14)*, to experience fullness of joy *(John 16:24)*, to know God's will *(Rom. 8:26-27)*, to find mercy and grace *(Heb. 4:16)*, and to offer sacrifices to God *(Heb. 13:15)*.

Two more reasons to pray are to learn authority and to release God's power. In the beginning God granted authority and dominion to Adam. When Adam sinned and fell, he lost the authority God intended for all humanity. But Jesus' sinless life and sacrificial death made it possible for us to recover all that Adam lost. As believers, we are now seated with Christ and are joint heirs with Him. God is in the process of restoring our authority by training us to use our authority properly. In eternity we will exercise that authority by reigning with Christ (see *Rev. 5:10*).

Because prayer is God's training ground, another reason we pray is to learn authority. We learn proper authority when we pray rightly and God answers. We learn wrong uses of authority when we pray incorrectly and God refuses our request.

Authority controls power. When you learn to use authority properly, you

REVELATION 5:10
"You have made them to be a kingdom and priests to serve our God, and they will reign on earth."

10 REASONS TO PRAY
1. **To spend time with God—the One you love**
2. **To identify with God by becoming like Him**

release God's power in answer to prayer. Exercising your authority in prayer releases God's power.

⚡ What are two reasons to pray?

To learn _____

To release God's _____

Review in the margin the list of reasons to pray. Ask the Lord which reason you need to emphasize most in your life today. Spend a few minutes in prayer for that reason.

Day 2
Daily Prayer

Because prayer is a relationship with God, prayer can actually be continual (see *1 Thess. 5:17; Heb. 13:15*). You need to live your life in such an attitude that you can talk to God anytime. You always need to listen so that He can speak to you at any time. God is always present with you as a believer. Therefore, you can pray continually.

⚡ Read the following Scriptures.

Look to the Lord and his strength; seek his face always (1 Chron. 16:11).

Jesus told his disciples a parable to show them that they should always pray and not give up (Luke 18:1).

Pray in the Spirit on all occasions with all kinds of prayers and requests. With this in mind, be alert and always keep on praying for all the saints (Eph. 6:18).

⚡ According to these Scriptures, how often should a believer pray during a day?
- ❑ Ten minutes in the morning and a blessing at each meal
- ❑ Three times a day, 15 minutes each time
- ❑ One hour a day
- ❑ Always, continually

3. To identify with God by working together with Him
4. To gain strength to resist temptation
5. To be made right with God
6. To find forgiveness, mercy, and grace
7. To learn God's will
8. To offer sacrifices to God
9. To learn authority
10. To release God's power

TODAY'S PRAYER PROMISE
"You did not choose me, but I chose you and appointed you to go and bear fruit—fruit that will last. Then the Father will give you whatever you ask in my name"
(John 15:16).

1 THESSALONIANS 5:17
"Pray continually."

HEBREWS 13:15
"Through Jesus, therefore, let us continually offer to God a sacrifice of praise."

You can always be in a spirit of prayer because you have a never-ending relationship with God.

JESUS' EXAMPLE

"Very early in the morning, while it was still dark, Jesus got up, left the house and went off to a solitary place, where he prayed" (Mark 1:35).

"After leaving them, he went up on a mountain-side to pray. When evening came, . . . he was alone on land" (Mark 6:46-47).

"Jesus often withdrew to lonely places and prayed" (Luke 5:16).

"Jesus went out to a mountainside to pray, and spent the night praying to God" (Luke 6:12).

Did you check *Always, continually?* Does that seem impossible? It is . . . if you see prayer as a religious activity that you perform at certain times each day. God created you for a relationship with Him. He is always present and can speak to you anytime. You can pray anytime. You can always be in a spirit of prayer because you have a never-ending relationship with God.

Try to envision a day in which you pray continually. You awake in the morning and thank God for a new day. You take time to be alone with Him. You read a passage from your Bible, through which God speaks to you. You spend time in confession, praise, worship, and thanksgiving. You talk to God about your life, what you need, and what He wants you to be. You pray for others and seek God's work in them and the circumstances they face. After you say, "Amen," are you finished praying for today? No, you shouldn't be.

You continue to listen to God and pray as you shower. You thank Him for your food and His blessings as you eat breakfast. On your way to school you pray for God's involvement in your school, for problems, for relationships, and for witnessing opportunities. While you are praying, your attention is captured by the beauty of a tree's leaves that are turning colors, and you worship God for the beauty of the earth and for His grandeur in creating it. A problem arises at school and you whisper a prayer to your Master in heaven for guidance. He guides you to resolve the problem, and you thank Him. A friend mentions a family problem, and you pray with her. You continue to commune with God throughout the day until bedtime, when you thank Him for the blessings of the day.

Think about a typical day. When are natural times to approach your Heavenly Father in prayers of confession, praise, worship, thanksgiving, petition, and intercession? List at least six times.

_____   _____

_____   _____

_____   _____

Spend today or tomorrow in an attitude of prayer all day, recognizing that God is always present. Be alert to times and ways you can pray privately as well as with others.

Times and Places to Pray

You can pray anytime and anywhere. Sometimes you can pray aloud, and sometimes you must pray silently. No one can prevent you from praying, even in a place where public pray is not permitted, because God is always present with you.

Many believers begin the day with a quiet time with God in prayer. Daniel prayed three times a day (see *Dan. 6:10*). Try to spend concentrated time in prayer, whether morning, noon, or evening. For these regular times of private prayer, find a place where you can be alone with God.

Take a few moments to pray about your personal prayer life. Ask God to direct you to make the adjustments necessary to develop a meaningful lifestyle of prayer.

DANIEL 6:10
"When Daniel learned that the decree [a law against prayer] had been published, he went home to his upstairs room where the windows opened toward Jerusalem. Three times a day he got down on his knees and prayed, giving thanks to his God, just as he had done before."

Day 3
Tools to Help You Pray

Y ou may have some simple yet practical questions about prayer. The remaining lessons this week will give you suggestions for developing your personal prayer life. Today we will share with you some tools we have used that may help in your personal prayer life.

TODAY'S PRAYER PROMISE
"Everything is possible for him who believes" *(Mark 9:23).*

Using a Prayer List, Notebook, or Computer

Organizing your thoughts in prayer is one way to show your reverence for God (see *Eccl. 5:2*). A prayer list may help you cover all of the areas for which you need to pray. You may want to keep a list in your Bible, or use a prayer journal like *DiscipleHelps: A Daily Quiet Time Guide and Journal* (available from the Sunday School Board by calling 1-800-458-2772), or use a computer file to guide your praying.

ECCLESIASTES 5:2
"Do not be quick with your mouth, do not be hasty in your heart to utter anything before God."

DAILY LIST
My mother
_____
_____

📑 Read the following descriptions of prayer lists. After you read about a list, write in the margin examples of a person, concern, or topic that you would include on your own list. We have given you a sample for each list.

Daily list. Keep a list of persons and subjects you pray for daily. Include members of your family, your pastor, several close friends, those in authority over you, and several continuing concerns.

Daily temporary list. Keep a daily temporary list of persons and concerns that change from time to time. Include special projects you are working on, sick

DAILY TEMPORARY LIST
Josh—father has cancer
_____
_____

WEEKLY LISTS
Monday: The Jones,
missionaries in Chile

_____

_____

MONTHLY LISTS
15th: My youth
group—unity

_____

_____

CONFESSION LIST
You are my Father; I am
Your child

_____

_____

PRAISE LIST
"Because your love is
better than life, my lips
will glorify you"
_(Ps. 63:3)._

_____

_____

WORSHIP LIST
"Worthy is the Lamb, who
was slain, to receive power
and wealth and wisdom
and strength and honor
and glory and praise!"
(Rev. 5:12).

_____

THANKSGIVING LIST
Salvation, privilege to
serve,

_____

_____

_____

friends, and other temporary requests.

Weekly lists. Each day of the week make a separate list of concerns you pray for on the same day each week. These weekly lists should include friends, church concerns, upcoming projects, governments, elected officials, and missionaries.

Monthly lists. For each day of the month (1-31) make a list that includes items of importance or concern but somewhat removed from your immediate situation. Pray for the items you have listed for each day of the month.

Confession, praise, worship, and thanksgiving lists. You may want to keep separate lists to use daily in your responding prayers. On these lists you might record attributes of God, items for which you are thankful, truths you want to confess, and so forth.

Scriptures. For many items on your lists you may want to write appropriate Scriptures. For example, write Scriptures that apply to a Christian friend as you pray for your friend. Choose other Scriptures that guide your praying for your pastor, missionaries, Christian leaders, and others.

Using your lists. Do not follow your lists so rigorously that the practice becomes legalistic, routine, or ritualistic. Prayer must be personal and intimate. Use your lists as general guides to:
- prevent your praying from focusing exclusively on yourself;
- aid your memory so that you do not forget special concerns;
- assign an order of importance to your requests if time is limited.

Also plan free periods of prayer in which you joyfully follow the Holy Spirit's leading in many matters, including concerns, praise, and thanksgiving. Be sensitive to ways your Father guides you to pray and listen for direction from your Master. During these times God may remind you of a person or a need not on your lists. These occasions can become special times of intercession.

Other Prayer Tools
All you need for prayer is the Lord's presence. However, you can use certain tools to enrich your prayer time. You may want to use a hymnal in prayer, for many hymn texts are prayers to God. You can pray a song or hymn to the Lord.

Many people like to use a journal (like _DiscipleHelps_) for writing their prayers to the Lord. Writing your prayers can help you focus on your requests and can remind you of your prayer when the answer comes. You may also want to use books on prayer, biographies of great people of prayer, maps, pictures, or other reminders for prayer.

As you pray to close this lesson, use the items you included on your lists in the margins as subjects for your prayers. You may want to begin your own notebook today for recording similar lists.

Day 4
The Bible and Prayer

Years ago I reached a point in my morning devotions at which I gave large blocks of time to prayer and only a few minutes to Bible study. Then I heard E. F. Hallock, a great preacher, say that we should not have to choose between time in the Bible and time in prayer. If a choice has to be made, it is more important that God speak to the individual than that a person speak to God. That statement reformed my prayer life. I began reading, studying, memorizing, and meditating on Scriptures more frequently. I found myself and my prayers increasingly being shaped by the words of Scripture that had become lodged in my subconscious.

Bible reading and study do not have to be separate activities from prayer. The Bible is another way God speaks. Therefore, prayer and Bible reading should be practiced together. Listen to what God may want to say to you as you read and study your Bible. Let the Scriptures point you to your love relationship with God.

> Read *John 5:39-40* in the margin. Where will a study of the Scriptures lead you?
> ❑ I find eternal life in a study of the Scriptures.
> ❑ The Scriptures lead me to knowledge of good literature.
> ❑ The Scriptures point me to a long list of do's and don'ts.
> ❑ The Scriptures point me to a love relationship with Jesus.

Jesus was speaking to the Pharisees in *John 5:39-40.* They knew that studying the Scriptures was important. Yet they had so emphasized and prided themselves in gaining knowledge that they missed the whole purpose—a love relationship with God through His Son, Jesus Christ. You too need to emphasize studying, reading, memorizing, and meditating on Scriptures. But don't place your focus on knowledge alone. Always look through the Scriptures to God. The Scriptures will lead you to Jesus, and He gives you life. He is your life!

Memorizing and meditating on (or thinking about) Scriptures are also valuable activities for your devotional life.

> Read *Joshua 1:8; Psalm 119:11,105* in the margin. When should you meditate on Scriptures?

TODAY'S PRAYER PROMISE
"If you believe, you will receive whatever you ask for in prayer"
(Matt. 21:22).

JOHN 5:39-40
"You diligently study the Scriptures because you think that by them you possess eternal life. These are the Scriptures that testify about me, yet you refuse to come to me to have life."

JOSHUA 1:8
"Do not let this Book of the Law depart from your mouth; meditate on it day and night, so that you may be careful to do everything written in it. Then you will be prosperous and successful."

PSALM 119:11
"I have hidden your word in my heart that I might not sin against you."

PSALM 119:105
"Your word is a lamp to my feet and a light for my path."

What is one reason for memorizing God's Word?

_____

What is a practical way God's Word can help you?

_____

    The Bible is a practical guide for living. It shows you God's will and God's ways. One reason for memorizing God's Word is so that you will not sin against God. When you know what God says about an activity or a relationship, you can obey what He commands. Meditating on the Scriptures you have memorized can also help you _observe_ and _do_ what God says. These Scriptures should be the subject of your thinking day and night. Scriptures are very valuable in shaping and guiding your prayer life. Here are some ways you might want to use Scriptures in your prayers.

WAYS TO USE SCRIPTURES IN PRAYER
- Quote a promise as assurance of an answer.
- Quote a fulfilled promise as a reason for praise.
- Apply Bible verses to a current situation.
- Use Bible verses as a prayer or praise.
- Use Bible phrases in a prayer.

Ask the Holy Spirit to guide you in applying Scriptures to a particular situation.

    As you use Scriptures in prayer, ask the Holy Spirit to guide you in applying them to a particular situation.

◪ Who has the right to decide which promises or Scriptures apply to situations for which you are praying?

❑ I do. If I find a Scripture I like, I can claim it as a promise and pressure God to do what I want.

❑ The Holy Spirit does. Only He knows God's mind and will. When He gives me a Scripture, I can depend on God to keep His Word.

    The Holy Spirit will guide you in using Scriptures to pray. Trust Him to help you when you don't know what to pray. He is ready to help you.

Close today's lesson by praying through Psalm 139 in your Bible. Observe that the Scriptures can be a wonderful aid in prayer.

Day 5
Being a House of Prayer

Jesus taught His disciples to pray. Nearly all His teaching on prayer focused on corporate or group prayer, using words like you (plural), our, we, and us.

▶ Read the Model Prayer *(Matt. 6:9-13)* in the margin. Circle the words you, we, our, and us.

Jesus began the Model Prayer by saying: "This, then, is how you (plural) should pray: " 'Our Father. . . . Give us. . . . Forgive us, . . . as we. . . . And lead us . . .' " *(Matt. 6:9-13,* emphasis added). God intended for His people to pray together. He said:

> "My house will be called
> a house of prayer for all nations" (Isa. 56:7).

God wanted His house to be a house of prayer. In *Luke 19* Jesus wept over Jerusalem because the people had refused to accept Him—the One who could have brought them peace. Then He made His way to the temple. There Jesus drove out of the temple those who were buying and selling animals *"It is written,"* he said to them, " '*My house will be a house of prayer,' but you have made it a 'den of robbers' "* (v. 46). As Jesus continued to teach in the temple in the days that followed, the religious leaders made plans to destroy Him. Because God's people were no longer a house of prayer, they sought to destroy Jesus (God Himself) when He came to them. A church must be a house of prayer, or it may begin to oppose God and what He wants to accomplish.

▶ If God evaluated your church or youth group, would He say that you are a house of prayer, a people of prayer? Check the statement that best describes your church.
- ❏ Yes, prayer is our life. We devote extended times to prayer and can testify to many answers to prayer. We know how to pray effectively. People send or call in prayer requests to us because they know we pray.
- ❏ No, we do not pray together often. Most of our prayers are brief and general in nature. Only one person prays, and everyone else listens or prays silently. Our prayer meetings are poorly attended, and we seldom hear testimonies about answered prayer.

TODAY'S PRAYER PROMISE
"Before they call I will answer; while they are still speaking I will hear" (Isa. 65:24).

MATTHEW 6:9-13
"This, then, is how you should pray: " 'Our Father in heaven, hallowed be your name, your kingdom come, your will be done on earth as it is in heaven. Give us today our daily bread. Forgive us our debts, as we also have forgiven our debtors. And lead us not into temptation, but deliver us from the evil one.' "

THE EARLY CHURCH:
A House of Prayer
"They all joined together constantly in prayer" (Acts 1:14).

"They devoted themselves to the apostles' teaching and to the fellowship, to the breaking of bread and to prayer" (Acts 2:42).

"We [the apostles] will give our attention to prayer and the ministry of the world" (Acts 6:3-4).

"Peter was kept in prison, but the church was earnestly praying to God for him" (Acts 12:5).

JOHN 17:11,21,23
"Holy Father, protect them by the power of your name—the name you gave me—so that they may be one as we are one. . . . that all of them may be one, Father, just as you are in me and I am in you. May they also be in us so that the world may believe that you have sent me. . . . I in them and you in me. May they be brought to complete unity to let the world know that you sent me and have loved them even as you have loved me."

Perhaps you could not check either statement because your church falls somewhere between these two extremes. If you had to check no, we have some good news for you. The very fact that you are studying this course and are learning to pray together with other believers indicates that God is at work! He may be preparing to take you, your youth group, and your church to a deeper level of united prayer than you have ever known.

Observe what a praying church looks like. Read in the margin the Scriptures from Acts. Was the early church a house of prayer?

❑ Yes, prayer was their life.

❑ No, they did not pray together often.

Praying in Unity

The early Christians were a group of united believers who prayed earnestly. The importance of the disciples' unity is seen repeatedly in Jesus' great prayer in *John 17* (see *vv. 11,21,23*). Jesus wanted the disciples to be one, to be united with a single purpose and spirit. He wanted them to be united just as He and God the Father are united. When this kind of unity is expressed in the church, the world around will know and believe that Jesus was indeed sent from God. Is it possible that our inadequacies in reaching people for Christ are due in part to our lack of unity? Probably so.

Jesus promises Christians a special presence when they gather together to pray: *"If two of you on earth agree about anything you ask for, it will be done for you by my Father in heaven. For where two or three come together in my name, there am I with them" (Matt. 18:19-20).* Jesus desires that the church be unified and that it pray together. This is exactly what we see in the beginnings of the church. Both the unity and the praying of the church are conspicuous, along with the results of its unified praying.

The most powerful form of prayer available to the body of Christ is united prayer. *Matthew 18:19-20* emphasizes that the greater unity you present to God when you pray together, the greater the authority God invests in your prayer.

Would you join us in praying that God will help your church become a house of prayer that is pleasing to Him and is powerful in prayer? If you will, pray now for that result.

Suggestions for Praying Together This Week

When you pray together, individuals have a tendency to pray about several topics at one time. Pay special attention during this session to pray about one subject at a time. Take turns praying about that subject. One person may pray about the circumstances. Another may pray for the persons involved. Another may pray for God's glory, purpose, or will. One may claim a scriptural promise or recall a biblical pattern that seems to apply. Let the Holy Spirit guide your prayer on a topic. Continue to pray about that subject as long as God seems to guide the praying.

Week 3
Responding Prayers

This Week's Scripture-Memory Verse
"Through Jesus, therefore, let us continually offer to God a sacrifice of praise—the fruit of lips that confess his name" (Heb. 13:15).

This Week's Lessons
Day 1: Confession: Responding to God's Holiness
Day 2: Praise: Responding to God's Attributes
Day 3: Worship: Responding to God's Glory
Day 4: Thanksgiving: Responding to God's Riches
Day 5: Responding Together

Summary of Week 3
This week you will:
- identify aspects God has revealed about Himself: His holiness, His attributes, His glory, and His riches;
- learn how to respond in prayer to God's aspects;
- understand that the purpose of responding prayers is to help you become the person God has planned for you to be;
- become more like God as you begin to respond to Him in confession, praise, worship, and thanksgiving;
- study in detail the four types of responding prayers.
  — Confession: responding to God's holiness
  — Praise: responding to God's attributes
  — Worship: responding to God's glory
  — Thanksgiving: responding to God's riches

This Week's Prayer Focus: Worship
God has acted in history including your history. Because of His nature (attributes), God's actions reveal His glory—His beauty, His splendor, and His worth. God's glory is evidence of His attributes. For instance, you know that God is powerful (an attribute). When God shows His power by giving you victory in a situation, He reveals His glory. The same is true when God reveals His love, mercy, forgiveness, justice, and other qualities. When God reveals His Person this way, you love Him and long to be with Him. You respond to God's glory through prayers of worship. You worship by expressing your reverence, honor, love, and adoration for God.

This week focus on the following Scriptures of worship. Worship the Lord, expressing your reverence and honor, your love and adoration.

Examples of Worship

"Yours, O Lord, is the greatness and the power
    and the glory and the majesty and
        the splendor,
    for everything in heaven and earth
        is yours.
Yours, O Lord, is the kingdom;
    you are exalted as head over all.
Wealth and honor come from you;
    you are the ruler of all things.
In your hands are strength and power
    to exalt and give strength to all"
        (1 Chron. 29:11-12).

As the deer pants for streams of water,
    so my soul pants for you, O God.
My soul thirsts for God, for the living God
        (Ps. 42:1-2).

All the nations you have made
    will come and worship before you, O Lord;
    they will bring glory to your name.
For you are great and do marvelous deeds;
    you alone are God (Ps. 86:9-10).

"You are worthy, our Lord and God,
    to receive glory and honor and power,
for you created all things,
    and by your will they were created
    and have their being" (Rev. 4:11).

"You are worthy to take the scroll
    and to open its seals,
because you were slain,
    and with your blood you purchased men
        for God
    from every tribe and language and people
        and nation."
"Worthy is the Lamb, who was slain,
to receive power and wealth and wisdom
        and strength
and honor and glory and praise!"
    (Rev. 5:9,12).

"Great and marvelous are your deeds,
    Lord God Almighty.
Just and true are your ways,
    King of the ages.
Who will not fear you, O Lord,
    and bring glory to your name?
For you alone are holy.
All nations will come
    and worship before you,
for your righteous acts have been revealed"
    (Rev. 15:3-4).

Come, let us bow down in worship,
    let us kneel before the Lord our Maker
        (Ps. 95:6).

Worship the Lord with gladness;
    come before him with joyful songs
        (Ps. 100:2).

"Let us go to his dwelling place;
    let us worship at his footstool"
        (Ps. 132:7).

Worship Commended

Ascribe to the Lord, O mighty ones,
    ascribe to the Lord glory and strength.
Ascribe to the Lord the glory due his name;
    worship the Lord in the splendor of his
        holiness (Ps. 29:1-2).

Day 1
Confession: Responding to God's Holiness

ISAIAH 6:1-3,5-7
I saw the Lord seated on a throne. . . . Above him were seraphs. . . . And they were calling to one another: "Holy, holy, holy is the Lord Almighty; the whole earth is full of his glory.

"Woe to me!" I cried. "I am ruined! For I am a man of unclean lips, and I live among a people of unclean lips, and my eyes have seen the King, the Lord Almighty."
Then one of the seraphs flew to me with a live coal in his hand, which he had taken with tongs from the altar. With it he touched my mouth and said, "See, this has touched your lips; your guilt is taken away and your sin atoned for."

God is holy. He is separate, pure, and righteous. God reveals His holiness because He wants you to be holy as He is holy: It is written: *"Be holy, because I am holy" (1 Pet. 1:16).* Yet we cannot be holy apart from God's work in us.

When God revealed Himself to persons in biblical accounts, one of the first qualities they recognized was His holiness.

Read in the margin about Isaiah's experience. Which of the following describes Isaiah's response to God's holiness?
❑ He realized his sin and cried out. He knew that his sin did not belong near God's holiness.
❑ He was proud to be in God's presence and boasted of his own goodness and righteousness.

How did God (through the seraphs) respond to Isaiah's cry?
❑ God killed Isaiah in His anger.
❑ God cleansed and forgave Isaiah in His love.

Confronted with God's holiness and purity, Isaiah cried out because of his sin. He agreed with what God already knew to be true. Isaiah had no reason to feel pride. God responded in love by taking away Isaiah's sin. Isaiah was cleansed and forgiven. After Isaiah had been prepared for God's presence, God talked with him about an assignment (see *Isa. 6:8-13*).

Confession

The Greek word for *confess* means *speak the same thing* or *agree with*. In one way all prayer is agreeing with God. Confession is agreeing with the truth. When you sin, God feels sadness or grief. You tend to feel guilty because of your sin. Satan, as the accuser of our brothers *(Rev. 12:10)*, reminds you of your sin so that you will feel guilty. Your guilt may cause you to run away or hide from God, as Adam and Eve did in the garden of Eden.

God wants you to agree with Him and return to a love relationship with Him. When you have a broken heart over your sin, you will want to do something about it: Godly sorrow brings repentance *(2 Cor. 7:10)*. Confession is agreeing with God about the real you and responding to God's holiness. Prayers of confession include seeking God's cleansing and forgiveness.

▶ How does God want you to feel about your sin?

Read *Proverbs 28:13* and *1 John 1:9* in the margin. Underline God's promises if we confess our sins.

Read *Hebrews 4:16* in the margin. How should we approach God to receive His mercy and grace?

The New Testament uses the word forgiveness in two ways. One is the legal sense of forgiveness. Jesus' death on the cross takes care of every sin a believer ever commits: past, present, and future. His sacrifice was all-sufficient. When you sin, you know it is already forgiven from a legal standpoint.

Sin in your life, however, stops the process of becoming like God. Sin breaks your fellowship and intimacy with God. *First John 1:9* speaks of the relational sense of forgiveness. When you respond to God's holiness by agreeing with Him about your sin, He promises to give mercy, forgiveness, and cleansing. He restores the relationship of intimacy. *Hebrews 4:16* encourages you to seek this mercy with confidence.

▶ Read *Hebrews 10:19,22* below. Notice how God's cleansing prepares you to enter His presence. Underline the words that describe the way you can enter His presence.

Since we have confidence to enter the Most Holy Place by the blood of Jesus, . . . let us draw near to God with a sincere heart in full assurance of faith, having our hearts sprinkled to cleanse us from a guilty conscience and having our bodies washed with pure water.

Because of Jesus you can enter God's presence with boldness and assurance. Develop the habit of agreeing with God so that when you sin, you immediately agree with Him about it and seek His forgiveness.

Pray, asking God to reveal sin in your life that hinders your relationship with Him. Use the sample prayer of confession in the margin to agree with God about your sin. Be specific. Seek God's cleansing and restoration. Ask Him to make you holy, as He is holy. Also see biblical examples of confession on pages 8-9.

PROVERBS 28:13
"He who conceals his sins does not prosper, but whoever confesses and renounces them finds mercy."

1 JOHN 1:9
"If we confess our sins, he is faithful and just and will forgive us our sins and purify us from all unrighteousness."

HEBREWS 4:16
"Let us then approach the throne of grace with confidence, so that we may receive mercy and find grace to help us in our time of need."

SAMPLE PRAYER OF CONFESSION
Lord, I don't feel what You feel, but I would like to. Help me feel the divine grief that You feel about my sin. Father, what I have done is not like You. And it is not like the real me that I am becoming in You. I want to agree with You about my sin and to become more like the real me, the eternal me that You want me to become. Cleanse me and restore me. Continue Your work in me. Make me holy, as You are holy. Amen.

Day 2
Praise: Responding to God's Attributes

EXAMPLES OF PRAISE
"I will give thanks to the Lord because of his righteousness" (Ps. 7:17).

"Be exalted, O Lord, in your strength; we will sing and praise your might" (Ps. 21:13).

"I trust in God's unfailing love for ever and ever. I will praise you forever for what you have done; in your name I will hope, for your name is good. I will praise you in the presence of your saints" (Ps. 52:8-9).

"Because your love is better than life, my lips will glorify you. I will praise you as long as I live" (Ps. 63:3-4).

"The heavens praise your wonders, O Lord, your faithfulness too" (Ps. 89:5).

According to yesterday's lesson, one kind of responding prayer that helps prepare you to enter the throne room of heaven in prayer is confession. Through confession you receive cleansing and are restored to a right relationship with God.

Confession is agreeing with God about the real you. You may object: "You don't know the real me. I don't want to be like the real me." Just one minute! The world tells you that you are a product of your past. If you agree with the world, that is the limit of the kind of person you will be—and that may not be very good. Christianity, however, teaches that you are a product of your future—what you are becoming. God is molding you into the image of His Son, Jesus Christ. As a Christian, you are becoming like Him. You are growing toward what you will be in eternity. Think of yourself in terms of eternity. This is the self about whom you want to agree with God in prayer.

Pause to pray. Fix in your mind an image of what Jesus is like—pure, loving, kind, holy, wise, humble, and gentle. Spend time in confession. Agree with God that the person you are becoming is more like Jesus in these ways.

A second kind of responding prayer is praise. In many different ways God reveals to you what He is like. His character traits are called His attributes. Praise is lifting up the attributes of God. You tend to become like what you value or praise. By lifting up God's attributes in prayer, you respond to God by becoming more like Him.

▶ Read in the margin the examples of praise. Pray them as you read. Circle God's attributes.

Do you see that praise focuses on who God is or what He is like? He is righteous, most high, strong and mighty, merciful, good, loving, wonderful, and faithful. These are just a few of God's attributes.

▶ Read the list of God's attributes in the margin on the next page. Underline the ones that are particularly meaningful to you.

Fill in the blanks to describe a second kind of responding prayer.

P _____ is responding to God's _____.

Which is the purpose of responding prayers like praise?
❑ I identify with God by working with Him in His Kingdom.
❑ I identify with God by becoming like Him.

When you pray, take time to offer praise to God. Respond to God's attributes by lifting them up. God wants you to become like Him. As you praise Him, ask Him to help you become more like Him. Allow God to remove every characteristic that is not like Him.

Praise is not just for the good times in your life. The writer of Hebrews said, *"Through Jesus, therefore, let us continually offer to God a sacrifice of praise"* (Heb. 13:15). Praising God for who He is and for what He is like should be an attitude of your heart. You can praise Him continually.

Paul and Silas, for example, were beaten and thrown into jail for taking a stand for Jesus Christ. Would you praise God at a time like that? Read what they did: *"About midnight Paul and Silas were praying and singing hymns to God, and the other prisoners were listening to them"* (Acts 16:25). Praise is insisting on the truth of God's nature regardless of the circumstances. God never changes. He is always worthy of our praise.

You will find that prayers of praise and worship (tomorrow's lesson) are closely related. Praise focuses on His attributes. Worship focuses on the evidence of His attributes—His glory. Praise and worship prayers blend together as you pray.

Using the attributes listed in this lesson and the biblical examples on pages 21-22, spend a few minutes praising God. You may want to use some of the biblical words for praise and worship below.

ATTRIBUTES OF GOD

Able, almighty, abounding in love, all-knowing, all-powerful, always present, attentive, awesome, beautiful, blameless, blessed, compassionate, consuming fire, enthroned, eternal, ever-present, exalted, faithful, first, flawless, forgiving, gentle, glorious, good, gracious, has authority, has integrity, healing, holy, indescribable, invisible, jealous, just, kind, last, light, living, majestic, merciful, mighty, patient, peaceful, perfect, protective, pure, radiant, righteous, slow to anger, spirit, strong, supreme, sure, tender, true, understanding, unfailing love, unique, wise, wonderful, worthy of praise

BIBLICAL WORDS FOR PRAISE AND WORSHIP

Praise	Hallelujah	Alleluia	Hosanna	Magnify
Exalt	Rejoice	Exult	Ascribe	Bless
Laud	Worship	Adore	Honor	Glorify

Day 3
Worship: Responding to God's Glory

TODAY'S PRAYER PROMISE
*"Open wide your mouth
and I will fill it"
(Ps. 81:10).*

a third kind of responding prayer is *worship*. In the New Testament the Greek word for *worship* derives from root words meaning *to kiss toward*. It is an act of homage, reverence, or love.

➤ **List the first three kinds of responding prayers.**

1. C _____

2. P _____

3. W _____

God's actions reveal His glory.

God is not like any other. He reveals to us His beauty, brightness, and splendor—His glory—as He shows His attributes. God's actions reveal His glory. The Bible indicates that the heavens and the earth declare God's glory. Creation is the evidence of God's great creative power, His beauty, His wisdom, and much more.

You respond to God's glory through prayers of worship.

When God reveals His glory, you recognize His worth—His surpassing value. You want to fall down and worship Him, love Him, and adore Him. You long to be with Him. You respond to God's glory through prayers of worship. You worship by expressing your reverence, honor, love, and adoration for God.

Read in the margin on the next page some prayers of worship from the Bible. Pray them as you read them. Think of God's beauty and majesty as you pray.

➤ **Write your own one-sentence prayer of worship.**

_____

Prayers of worship and praise go together. As you pray, you will find yourself focusing on God's attributes and praising Him. When you reflect on who God is and how He has revealed Himself, you will worship and adore Him. Worship begins with reverence for God.

Here are some ways you can express prayers of worship.

1. Describe your holy reverence for God. Acknowledge and honor His presence. Do not treat God's presence casually or lightly.
2. Magnify the Lord. Make Him bigger. The word *magnify* indicates perspective. You cannot make God bigger than He is. However, when you decrease yourself and magnify Him, He increases. That is what Mary did when she prayed: *"My soul doth magnify the Lord. For he hath regarded the low estate of his handmaiden" (Luke 1:46,48,* KJV). Focus on God's greatness in comparison to who you are.
3. Exalt the Lord. Make Him higher. John said of Jesus, *"He must become greater; I must become less" (John 3:30).*
4. Ascribe to the Lord the glory due Him. Give God proper credit for what He has done. Do not accept His glory as your own.
5. Bless the Lord. Speak well of Him.
6. Glorify the Lord. Give Him honor and glory in what you say.

◪ **Read in the margin the sample prayers of worship. Underline those that express your feelings of worship. Now pray them to the Lord.**

Prayers of worship are responses to God's glory. Because God is Spirit, you must worship God in spirit. The opposite of spirit is flesh, which can taint worship when you focus on self. Pride and arrogance before God prevent true worship. The real test in worship is this: Who is first? Who is foremost? To worship in spirit, think of God first. Seek to meet God, to see Him, to think about Him to please Him, to fix your mind on Him. Flesh will lead you astray. Spirit will always lead you to God's supremacy. God's glory is very sacred. You dare not give His glory to another or take it for yourself, for God said:

> *"I am the Lord; that is my name!*
> *I will not give my glory to another" (Isa. 42:8).*

God's glory, demonstrated in your life, is the greatest good that can come to you. His glory is best demonstrated when your life reflects His character. The way you live your life can demonstrate worship to God by glorifying Him. God wants you to attain maturity, to reach the measure of the stature of Christ, and to become complete in Christ. When you worship the Lord, God works in you to make you more like Him.

EXPRESSING PRAYERS OF WORSHIP

1. Describe your reverence for God.
2. Magnify the Lord.
3. Exalt the Lord.
4. Ascribe to the Lord the glory due Him.
5. Bless the Lord.
6. Glorify the Lord.

SAMPLE PRAYERS OF WORSHIP

- Honor and majesty belong to You.
- I stand in awe of Your greatness and power.
- I love You because You first loved me.
- I long to be with You, Lord. I hunger and thirst for You.
- I would rather be a doorkeeper in Your house than live as a rich person with the wicked.
- The heavens declare Your glory, Lord. I worship You in the splendor of Your holiness.
- The earth is full of Your glory, Lord. Your wisdom, knowledge, and power are beyond my understanding.
- I long to be with You in eternity. I yearn for my redemption to be complete in Christ.
- I desire intimate fellowship with You.

Close today's study by worshiping the Lord. Focus on Him as you express your reverence, awe, love, and adoration. Use the words at the end of day 2 if you wish.

Day 4
Thanksgiving: Responding to God's Riches

TODAY'S PRAYER PROMISE
"Every good and perfect gift is from above, coming down from the Father"
(Jas. 1:17).

God is our source for abundant living.

EPHESIANS 1:3-9,11
Praise be to the God and Father of our Lord Jesus Christ, who has blessed us in the heavenly realms with every spiritual blessing in Christ. For he chose us in him before the creation of the world to be holy and blameless in his sight. In love he predestined us to be adopted as his sons through Jesus Christ, in accordance with his pleasure and will—to the praise of his glorious

Squeezing toothpaste onto my toothbrush one morning, I realized that I had never thanked God for toothpaste. Come to think of it, I had never thanked Him for my teeth. I wondered: *What if my blessings tomorrow depended on my thanksgiving today? It would mean that if I did not thank God for air and lungs today, there would be no air tomorrow, and my lungs would collapse!*

Few of us realize our total dependence on God. We fail to acknowledge God as the source of everything we have. He is our source for abundant living, bestowing on us material and spiritual blessings according to His grace.

▶ Read today's prayer promise, *James 1:17*. Where does every good and perfect gift come from?

_____

Read *Ephesians 1:3-9,11* in the margin and underline some spiritual blessings God has given you.

Every good gift comes from God. He has blessed you with all spiritual blessings. God has adopted you as a child, has forgiven your sins, has given you wisdom and judgment, has revealed His will, and has given you an inheritance.

When God reveals Himself by giving blessings to you, thanksgiving to Him is a natural response. Thanksgiving is not just an act or a statement. It is an attitude of gratitude. Thanksgiving indicates a relationship between God as source and you as receiver. Prayers of thanksgiving indicate one of the most important characteristics of your relationship with God. Your relationship can grow only when you properly acknowledge that you are the receiver and God is the Giver.

▶ Read *Ephesians 5:20* and *Philippians 4:6* below.

> *... always giving thanks to God the Father for everything, in the name of our Lord Jesus Christ (Eph. 5:20).*

> *In everything, by prayer and petition, with thanksgiving, present your requests to God (Phil. 4:6).*

What does Paul say about gratitude?
❑ Thank God for only the good things in life.
❑ Thank God in every situation—both good and difficult.
❑ Thanksgiving is not important unless you want something.

Paul tells us always to be thankful in every situation. This is difficult for most of us. We think of gratitude merely as a reaction to a favor, not to unpleasant events. Properly expressing gratitude means that you thank God in all circumstances—large and small, good and bad. Response to God in gratitude should be a continuous attitude of your heart. *Give thanks in all circumstances, for this is God's will for you in Christ Jesus (1 Thess. 5:18).*

Learning to be content in whatever state in which you find yourself helps you submit to God's sovereignty. He wants you to develop gratitude for all you have rather than to focus on what you do not have. Thanksgiving is responding to God for the blessings He has bestowed on you.

Gratitude is a continuous attitude about your relationship with the One who continuously gives to you, supplies your needs, and brings you joy. Gratitude is a response not only to what God does but also to who God is. Gratitude is the heart's response to God's goodness—not merely to the gifts of His goodness but also to His quality of goodness.

▶ What quality of God encourages our gratitude?

_____

_____

Turn to pages 47-48 and read the examples of thanksgiving. List from Scripture some things for which you can thank God.

_____   _____

_____   _____

_____   _____

grace, which he has freely given us in the One he loves. In him we have redemption through his blood, the forgiveness of sins, in accordance with the riches of God's grace that he lavished on us with all wisdom and understanding. And he made known to us the mystery of his will according to his good pleasure, which he purposed in Christ.

In him we were also chosen, having been predestined according to the plan of him who works out everything in conformity with the purpose of his will.

Gratitude is a response not only to what God does but also to who God is.

ROMANS 8:28

43

"In all things God works for the good of those who love him, who have been called according to his purpose."

God's nature is good. His will and work are always good. You can thank God for even the difficult or trying experiences in life, knowing that He can work through those for your good (see *Rom. 8:28* in the margin). Here are some other things for which you can thank God: spiritual riches, honor, strength, His nearness, His wonderful works, joy and gladness, freedom, daily provision, a call to be involved in His work, and wisdom.

SUBJECTS FOR THANKS
- Redemption, mercy, grace, forgiveness
- Meaningful spiritual experiences
- Family, relatives, friends, and church
- Provision for your needs
- Persons and events that have had spiritual impacts on your life

◪ Read in the margin the list of subjects for thanks. List other things, persons, or experiences for which you can give thanks.

_____   _____

_____   _____

Pray through your lists, expressing your gratitude to God for His goodness and for all He is and does for you. Be alert to ways to express your gratitude to God today.

Day 5
Responding Together

You will spend most of this week's prayer session in responding prayers. Today you will prepare for your group prayer session.

TODAY'S PRAYER PROMISE
"Come now, let us reason together," says the Lord. "Though your sins are like scarlet, they shall be as white as snow; though they are red as crimson, they shall be like wool" (Isa. 1:18).

Preparing to Confess

In *Isaiah 1:18*, today's prayer promise, God invites you to reason together with Him about your sin. No matter how bad the sin appears, He can cleanse and forgive! Confession is a way to respond to God's holiness by agreeing with Him and turning away from your sin. As you do, God makes you holy—set apart for His work.

Sometimes sin needs to be confessed publicly (see *Neh. 9:1-3* in the margin for an example). This is especially true when a group has sinned. We call this corporate sin.

NEHEMIAH 9:1-3
The Israelites gathered together, fasting and wearing sackcloth and having dust on their heads. Those of Israelite descent had separated themselves from

▶ Circle sins that could be church sins or group sins rather than individual sins. Some could be both.

Pride	Murder	Robbery	Sexual immorality
Envy	Adultery	Bribery	Tolerating evil
Greed	Unbelief	Unforgiveness	Shifting priority from God
Lying	Gossip	Bitterness	Neglecting the needy

Nearly all of these could be sins of a church or a group. Some, however, like murder, robbery, sexual immorality, adultery, bribery, lying, and gossip, are more likely to be individual sins. *James 5:16*, in the margin, commands us to confess our faults to one another. Healing and deliverance can come when others pray for you about an area of sin, weakness, need, or fault. Take care, however, when you confess sin publicly. Below are some guidelines to follow when confessing sin to others.

Guidelines for Confession

1. Confession should be directed by the Holy Spirit.
2. Limit confession to what is corporately (as a group) agreed on as sin.
3. Corporate confession is not accusation of others but agreement with God and with one another.
4. Confession includes sins of omission and commission.
5. The purpose of confessing personal sin is to secure forgiveness or to enlist prayer support.
6. Any sin that causes damage to a group should be publicly confessed.
7. The circle of confession should be as wide as the circle of damage done by the sin.
8. Confession should not be public when it would hurt other persons or lead to anger or lust.

Confession also includes agreeing with God about truth.

▶ Turn to page 9 and read two examples of confession of truth. Now read in the margin the list of sample prayers of the confession of truth. On the lines provided, list other truths you can confess about God or about who you are in relation to God.

_____

_____

_____

all foreigners. They stood in their places and confessed their sins and the wickedness of their fathers. They stood where they were and read from the Book of the Law of the Lord their God for a quarter of the day, and spent another quarter in confession and in worshiping the Lord their God.

JAMES 5:16
Confess your sins to each other and pray for each other so that you may be healed. The prayer of a righteous man is powerful and effective.

SAMPLE PRAYERS OF THE CONFESSION OF TRUTH
- **Sin no longer has dominion over me.**
- **You have dressed me in robes of Your righteousness.**
- **You are Lord and Master; I am Your servant.**
- **You are my Father; I am Your child.**
- **You are Sovereign; my answer is yes.**
- **You are Truth; You are my Way and Life.**
- **I walk in victory with Christ.**
- **Greater is He who is in me than he who is in the world.**

Preparing to Praise

During your group prayer time this week you will respond to God's attributes in praise. You might use statements like these: "I praise You, Lord, for You are. . . ." "I magnify Your name because You are. . . ."

▶ List four or more attributes of God for which you can praise Him. If you need to, scan Psalms to find some of His attributes.

_____   _____

_____   _____

Preparing to Worship

▶ Turn to pages 34-35 and select a passage that is meaningful to you. Write the reference here:

_____

What does this passage reveal about God's glory?

_____

_____

Preparing to Give Thanks

▶ Review the lists on pages 43-44 of things for which you can express thanks.

Spend a few minutes in prayer, responding to God's holiness, attributes, glory, and riches.

 Week 4
Asking Prayers

This Week's Scripture-Memory Verse
Do not be anxious about anything, but in everything, by prayer and petition, with thanksgiving, present your requests to God (Phil. 4:6).

This Week's Lessons
Day 1: Praying for Yourself and Others
Day 2: Reasons God Answers Prayer
Day 3: Reasons God Does Not Answer Prayer
Day 4: Principles for Asking
Day 5: Agreeing Together

Summary of Week 4
This week begins a focus on asking prayers: petition and intercession. Jesus taught much about asking prayers. This week you will:
- understand the importance of asking and of agonizing in prayer;
- consider biblical examples to identify reasons God does and does not answer prayer;
- apply biblical truths to improve the effectiveness of your prayer life;
- understand basic principles for asking prayers;
- learn how to pray in agreement with others as you pray together.

This Week's Prayer Focus: Thanksgiving
God is our source for abundant living. He bestows on us material and spiritual blessings according to His grace. When God reveals Himself by giving blessings to you, thanksgiving is a natural response. Thanksgiving is responding to God's blessings. Thanksgiving is not just an act or a statement. It is an attitude of gratitude. Prayers of thanksgiving reveal a relationship between the giver and the receiver.

This week focus on the following Scriptures of thanksgiving. Express to the Lord your gratitude. Thank Him for all He has done for you.

Examples of Thanksgiving

Wealth and honor come from you;
you are the ruler of all things.
In your hands are strength and power
to exalt and give strength to all.
Now, our God, we give you thanks,
and praise your glorious name
(1 Chron. 29:12-13).

You turned my wailing into dancing;
you removed my sackcloth and clothed me
with joy,
that my heart may sing to you and not
be silent.
O Lord my God, I will give you thanks
forever (Ps. 30:11-12).

We give thanks to you, O God,
we give thanks, for your Name is near;
men tell of your wonderful deeds
(Ps. 75:1).

O Lord, truly I am your servant;
I am your servant, the son of your
maidservant;
you have freed me from my chains.
I will sacrifice a thank offering to you
and call on the name of the Lord
(Ps. 116:16-17).

"We give thanks to you, Lord God Almighty,
the One who is and who was,
because you have taken your great power
and have begun to reign" (Rev. 11:17).

Daniel's Prayers of Thanksgiving

I thank and praise you, O God of my fathers:
You have given me wisdom and power,
you have made known to me what
we asked of you (Dan. 2:23).

Three times a day [Daniel] got down on his
knees and prayed, giving thanks to his God
(Dan. 6:10).

Jesus' Prayers of Thanksgiving

Jesus then took the loaves, gave thanks, and
distributed to those who were seated as much
as they wanted (John 6:11).

Jesus looked up and said, "Father, I thank you that
you have heard me" (John 11:41).

Paul's Prayers of Thanksgiving

I have not stopped giving thanks for you,
remembering you in my prayers (Eph. 1:16).

I thank Christ Jesus our Lord, who has given
me strength, that he considered me faithful,
appointing me to his service (1 Tim. 1:12).

A Call to Thanksgiving

Give thanks to the Lord, call on his name;
make known among the nations what
he has done (Ps. 105:1).

Give thanks to the Lord, for he is good;
his love endures forever (Ps. 107:1).

Do not be anxious about anything, but in
everything, by prayer and petition, with

thanksgiving, present your requests to God
(Phil. 4:6).

Give thanks in all circumstances, for this is
God's will for you in Christ Jesus (1 Thess. 5:18).

Day 1
Praying for Yourself and Others

You have now completed half of your study of *In God's Presence*. Let's review what you have learned.

SCRIPTURE-MEMORY VERSE
"Do not be anxious about anything, but in everything, by prayer and petition, with thanksgiving, present your requests to God" (Phil. 4:6).

Can you recite your three memory verses? Check the boxes beside the verses you can recite successfully.
❏ *John 15:17*   ❏ *Matthew 18:19*   ❏ *Hebrews 13:15*

Name four kinds of responding prayers and the aspects of God's nature to which you respond. Check your answers on page 95.

_____ is responding to God's _____
_____ is responding to God's _____
_____ is responding to God's _____
_____ is responding to God's _____

What is the purpose of responding prayers?
❏ I identify with God by working with Him in His Kingdom.
❏ I identify with God by becoming like Him.

What are two kinds of asking prayers?
_____ is asking for myself that is led by my Father.
_____ is asking for others that is led by my Master.

Which of the following is the purpose of asking prayers?
❏ I identify with God by working with Him in His Kingdom.
❏ I identify with God by becoming like Him.

We have studied four types of responding prayers. In confession, praise, worship, and thanksgiving you identify with God by becoming like Him. Now we will focus on asking prayers: petition and intercession. In asking prayers you identify with God by working with Him in His Kingdom.

God's Way of Working

Many years ago when I served in the Korean War, I learned that very few Koreans were Christians at that time—less than 1 percent. But they prayed fervently and faithfully. Prayer was their very life. Today over 29 percent of Koreans are Christians. Do you know why? Because they are praying, and God is answering. In fact, they may be the most prayerful people in the world. God is honoring their prayers.

All around the world God is moving. He is moving mightily where people are praying. Do you know what the problem is where people are not responding to the gospel? The body of Christ is in poor condition. We are not praying. We are not seeing the great work of God. God's work must be done on God's basis. That is the only way He will work. Jesus repeatedly emphasized the method for accomplishing God's work; we must ask.

GOD INVITES ASKING

"Ask and it will be given to you; seek and you will find; knock and the door will be opened to you" (Matt. 7:7).

"You may ask me for anything in my name, and I will do it" (John 14:14).

"If you remain in me and my words remain in you, ask whatever you wish, and it will be given you" (John 15:7).

"Until now you have not asked for anything in my name. Ask and you will receive, and your joy will be complete" (John 16:24).

▶ **Read the Scriptures in the margin. Circle the word ask in each verse.**

Real prayer is difficult. We are so comfortable, however, that we don't want to fight. We are failing in kingdom work because we are not fighting. Paul begged the Roman Christians *to join me in my struggle by praying to God for me (Rom. 15:30).* In writing to the Colossian church, Paul said, *"[Epaphras] is always wrestling in prayer for you, that you may stand firm in all the will of God, mature and fully assured" (Col. 4:12).* I don't know very many who strive or wrestle in prayer. Not only do we need individual prayer warriors today, but we also need churches that are houses of prayer.

▶ **Check the better description of the kind of prayer needed today.**
❑ We need prayer that is easy. If little time or effort is required, many more people will agree to pray.
❑ We need agonizing and fervent prayer. Much time and great effort are required for the kind of results needed today.

The church needs agonizing and fervent prayer. Perhaps sin has become so common among God's people that God does not hear our prayers. Instead of getting right with God, we have stopped praying. We are not even asking. We are not achieving victories for Christ. We are not doing God's work on God's basis.

Ask God to begin showing you the kind of prayer He wants of you. Ask Him to stir your heart to agonizing and fervent prayer for His Kingdom's sake. Pray for your church to become a house of prayer.

Day 2
Reasons God Answers Prayer

The great prayer warriors of the Bible often told God why He should answer their prayers. Seeking God's viewpoint, they desired to pray for what God wanted to do. Today you will learn some reasons God answers prayer.

◨ Read the following eight reasons God answers prayer. Underline a word or two in each one to help you remember it.

1. *The prayer seeks to uphold God's honor.* God's honor means His good name, reputation, or integrity. In some prayers you may seek to maintain the integrity of God's character and His name.

   After the faithless report of the spies who were sent into the Promised Land, God threatened to slay the Israelites. Moses prayed on behalf of God's honor, expressing a desire to protect God's reputation among the surrounding nations (see *Num. 14:15-16*).

2. *The prayer appeals for God's glory.* God's glory invites worshipful praise. His glory is His magnificence, His great beauty or splendor, or the evidence of His attributes. In some prayers you may ask that God reveal or receive His glory. We dare not give His glory to another or take it for ourselves.

   The men and women of the Bible were always diligent to ensure that divine work was recognized as truly from God—they gave God the glory. Jesus prayed for His Father's glory (see *John 12:27-28*) instead of seeking His own desires.

3. *The prayer appeals to God's character.* God's character refers to His traits, qualities, or nature. You can agree with God about His nature in prayer. You can also ask Him to act according to His nature.

   Moses made a request based on God's character, identifying several of His qualities (see *Num. 14:17-19*). Because God is merciful, forgiving, and longsuffering, Moses asked God to pardon and forgive the people.

4. *The prayer acknowledges God's sovereignty.* God's sovereignty means His supreme power, rank, or authority over all. He is Ruler over all.

   As Sennacherib gathered his Assyrian army against King Hezekiah, Hezekiah acknowledged God's sovereignty over all kingdoms of the earth. He realized that a positive answer to his request would cause all of the kingdoms to recognize that truth as well (see *2 Kings 19:15,19*).

5. *Jesus prays for you.* Have you ever asked a godly person to pray for you,

TODAY'S PRAYER PROMISE
"In that day you will no longer ask me anything. I tell you the truth, my Father will give you whatever you ask in my name. Until now you have not asked for anything in my name. Ask and you will receive, and your joy will be complete" (John 16:23-24).

GOD'S HONOR
"If you put these people to death all at one time, the nations who have heard this report about you will say, 'The Lord was not able to bring these people into the land he promised them on oath; so he slaughtered them in the desert' " (Num. 14:15-6).

GOD'S GLORY
"Now my heart is troubled, and what shall I say? 'Father, save me from this hour'? No, it was for this very reason I came to this hour. Father, glorify your name" (John 12:27-28).

GOD'S CHARACTER

"As you have declared: 'The Lord is slow to anger, abounding in love and forgiving sin and rebellion.' . . . In accordance with your great love, forgive the sin of these people, just as you have pardoned them from the time they left Egypt until now" (Num. 14:17-19).

GOD'S SOVEREIGNTY

"O Lord, God of Israel, enthroned between the cherubim, you alone are God over all the kingdoms of the earth. . . . Now, O Lord our God, deliver us from his hand, so that all kingdoms on earth may know that you alone, O Lord, are God" (2 Kings 19:15,19).

MASTER-SERVANT

"May these words of mine . . . be near to the Lord our God day and night, that he may uphold the cause of his servant. . . so that all the peoples of the earth may know that the Lord is God and that there is no other" (1 Kings 8:59-60).

thinking that God would surely hear? You have an even better reason for God to answer your request: Jesus Himself prays for you! Paul tells us, "Christ *Jesus . . . is at the right hand of God and is also interceding for us" (Rom. 8:34).* Because Jesus is interested in you, He supports you in every appropriate prayer you utter and seeks God's very best for you.

6. **The Holy Spirit prays with and for you according to God's will.** Your greatest weakness in prayer may be that you do not know what or how to ask. But here's good news: *The Spirit helps us in our weakness. We do not know what we ought to pray for, but the Spirit himself intercedes for us . . . in accordance with God's will (Rom. 8:26-27).* The Holy Spirit knows God's will and guides you to pray according to God's will.

7. **Your Father wants to answer the requests of His child.** God answers prayer because of who you are in relation to Him. Jesus commanded you to pray to God as Father: " *'Our Father in heaven' " (Matt. 6:9).* Your relationship as a child of God ought to influence the way you pray. God hears you because you are His child.

8. **Your Master wants to answer the requests of His servant.** You can also pray on the basis of being God's servant. The cause of God cannot be separated from that of His servants. If you are His servant, your prayers touch His work and interest Him.

   After the dedication of the temple Solomon prayed as a servant to his Master (see *1 Kings 8:59-60*).

Pray and ask God to teach you how to pray from His viewpoint. List one of your most important prayer requests today. Review the eight reasons God answers prayer and state why God would want to answer your prayer. Ask God what He wants you to pray for. Then pray from God's viewpoint, stating His reasons for answering your request.

Prayer request: _____

Reasons for God to answer: _____

_____

_____

_____

Day 3
Reasons God Does Not Answer Prayer

any sin is serious and hinders prayer. We want to avoid all sin, but we are wise to give special attention to sins the Bible specifically identifies as hindrances to prayer.

Read the Scriptures in the margins on this page and on page 54 (*Ps. 66:18; Isa. 59:1-2; Heb. 3:12,18-19; Jas. 1:5-8; 4:2-3*). Underline reasons God doesn't answer prayer or actions that hinder prayer.

Below is a list of sins that are reasons God doesn't answer prayer, followed by a series of Scriptures. Match the sin with the Scripture that mentions it by writing one or more references under each sin.

Anger/wrath:
_____

Broken relationships:
_____

Doubting/unbelief:
_____

Hypocrisy:
_____

Idolatry:
_____

Indifference to need:
_____

Unforgiveness:
_____

"Son of man, these men have set up idols in their hearts and put wicked stumbling blocks before their faces. Should I let them inquire of me at all?" (Ezek. 14:3).

TODAY'S PRAYER PROMISE
We have confidence before God and receive from him anything we ask, because we obey his commands and do what pleases him (1 John 3:21-22).

PSALM 66:18
"If I had cherished sin in my heart, the Lord would not have listened."

ISAIAH 59:1-2
"Surely the arm of the Lord is not too short to save, nor his ear too dull to hear. But your iniquities have separated you from your God; your sins have hidden his face from you, so that he will not hear."

HEBREWS 3:12,18-19
"See to it, brothers, that none of you has a sinful, unbelieving heart that turns away from the living God. . . .To whom did God swear that they would never enter his rest if not to those who disobeyed? So we see that they were not able to enter, because of their unbelief."

JAMES 1:5-8

"If any of you lacks wisdom, he should ask God, who gives generously to all without finding fault, and it will be given to him. But when he asks, he must believe and not doubt, because he who doubts is like a wave of the sea, blown and tossed by the wind. That man should not think he will receive anything from the Lord; he is a double-minded man, unstable in all he does."

JAMES 4:2-3

"You want something but don't get it. You kill and covet, but you cannot have what you want. You quarrel and fight. You do not have, because you do not ask God. When you ask, you do not receive, because you ask with wrong motives, that you may spend what you get on your pleasures."

If a man shuts his ears to the cry of the poor,
    he too will cry out and not be answered (Prov. 21:13).

"If you are offering your gift at the altar and there remember that your brother has something against you, leave your gift there in front of the altar. First go and be reconciled to your brother; then come and offer your gift" (Matt. 5:23-24).

"When you pray, do not be like the hypocrites, for they love to pray standing in the synagogues and on the street corners to be seen by men. I tell you the truth, they have received their reward in full" (Matt. 6:5).

"If you forgive men when they sin against you, your heavenly Father will also forgive you. But if you do not forgive men their sins, your Father will not forgive your sins" (Matt. 6:14-15).

I will therefore that men pray every where, lifting up holy hands, without wrath and doubting (1 Tim. 2:8, KJV).

Husbands, in the same way be considerate as you live with your wives, and treat them with respect as the weaker partner and as heirs with you of the gracious gift of life, so that nothing will hinder your prayers (1 Pet. 3:7).

Answers: anger/wrath: *1 Timothy 2:8*; broken relationships: *Matthew 5:23-24; 1 Peter 3:7*; doubting/unbelief: *1 Timothy 2:8*; hypocrisy: *Matthew 6:5*; idolatry: *Ezekiel 14:3*; indifference to need: *Proverbs 21:13*; unforgiveness: *Matthew 6:14-15*.

Examine the following list of sins and hindrances to prayer. Ask God to show you any area of your life that may be a barrier in your prayer life. If He shows you anything, confess it. Seek His forgiveness and determine to walk in a new way. Check off each area as you allow God to examine it. Take as much time for this process as God may require.

- ❑ *Anger/wrath*
- ❑ *Doubting/unbelief*
- ❑ *Idolatry (idols of the heart)*
- ❑ *Iniquities (moral crookedness)*
- ❑ *Unforgiveness*

- ❑ *Broken relationships*
- ❑ *Hypocrisy*
- ❑ *Indifference to need*
- ❑ *Sins*
- ❑ *Wrong or selfish motives*

Day 4
Principles for Asking

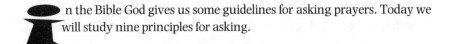 n the Bible God gives us some guidelines for asking prayers. Today we will study nine principles for asking.

▶ Read the Scriptures in the margins as you read the principles.

1. *Ask in the Spirit.* This means that every request proceeds from the mind of the Spirit, not from selfish motives or self-serving ends. Praying in the Spirit is directly related to praying according to His will.
2. *Ask according to His will.* Our weakness in prayer is this: *We do not know what we ought to pray for, but the Spirit himself intercedes for us . . . in accordance with God's will (Rom. 8:26-27).* Ask according to God's will with the help of the Holy Spirit. When you don't know what to ask, keep praying and seeking God's direction for your prayer.
3. *Ask with the mind.* Your mind helps you form your requests and make them precise and specific. This is one reason to list prayer requests in a journal like *DiscipleHelps.* A prayer list keeps your mind from wandering as you pray and enables you to pray specifically and persistently until the answer comes.

▶ List the first three principles of asking.

1. Ask in

   _____

2. Ask according to

   _____

3. Ask with

   _____

4. *Ask in Jesus' name.* When you use Jesus' name, you claim to represent Him and act like Him—to have His desires, qualities, gratitude, and outlook. When you prepare to make a request, first ask yourself, *What would Jesus want in this situation?* Let His desires become your desires. Praying in Jesus' name also relates to praying according to His will.

TODAY'S PRAYER PROMISE
"I will do whatever you ask in my name, so that the Son may bring glory to the Father. You may ask me for anything in my name, and I will do it" (John 14:13-14).

IN THE SPIRIT
I will pray with my spirit (1 Cor. 14:15).

Pray in the Spirit on all occasions (Eph. 6:18).

ACCORDING TO HIS WILL
"This is the confidence we have in approaching God: that if we ask anything according to his will, he hears us. And if we know that he hears us—whatever we ask—we know that we have what we asked of him" (1 John 5:14-15).

WITH THE MIND
"I will also pray with my mind" (1 Cor. 14:15).

IN JESUS' NAME
"You may ask me for anything in my name, and I will do it" (John 14:14).

ABIDING IN CHRIST

"If you remain in me and my words remain in you, ask whatever you wish, and it will be given you" (John 15:7).

IN FAITH

"Have faith in God. Whatever you ask for in prayer, believe that you have received it, and it will be yours" (Mark 11:22,24).

5. *Ask while abiding in Christ.* Prayer is both a means and a result of abiding in Christ. To abide in Him, you continue in constant fellowship with Him; you pray without ceasing; and you obediently accept His will and Word for you. As a branch abides in the vine, a Christian abides in Christ. Spend time with Him in prayer and in His Word.

6. *Ask in faith.* Asking in faith means asking without doubt in your heart. Believe that the things you ask will come to pass. Reflect God's character in always being the same. Recognize God's authority and power to answer in the way He chooses. Have confidence in God's care and purposes for your life. Finally, you can claim a God-given Bible promise and anticipate God's response.

⤵ List three more principles of asking.

    4. Ask in

    _____

    5. Ask according to

    _____

    6. Ask with

    _____

IN HUMILITY

"If my people, who are called by my name, will humble themselves and pray . . ." (2 Chron. 7:14).

IN SINCERITY

The prayer of a righteous man is powerful and effective (Jas. 5:16).

WITH PERSEVERANCE

Pray in the Spirit on all occasions with all kinds of prayers and requests. With this in mind, be alert and always keep on praying for all the saints (Eph. 6:18).

7. *Ask in humility.* Praying in humility recognizes your need of God. Humility submits to God, whereas pride, arrogance, and independence prevent an attitude of humility. The secret to humility is to understand who God is. Pride always indicates that you have failed to perceive His greatness. Come to God recognizing His greatness and your need.

8. *Ask in sincerity.* When you pray in sincerity, your faith leads you to pray genuine, heartfelt prayers. You are so serious about your praying that your prayer is earnest and fervent, not fake or artificial.

9. *Ask with perseverance. Perseverance* means *persistence, not giving up.* God expects you to persevere in prayer to make you sure of what He wants and of what you want. He wants to train you to take your eyes off discouraging circumstances and to focus on Him. He also wants you to prove and establish earnestness and to demonstrate real faith.

⤵ List the last three principles of asking.

    7. Ask in

    _____

8. Ask according to

   _____

9. Ask with

   _____

Review the nine principles for asking. You may want to write them on an index card for regular review. Now spend some time with your Father and Master in prayer. As you phrase your requests, practice the principles for asking. Begin keeping a list of your requests so that you can pray with your mind.

Day 5
Agreeing Together

When your church or group prays together, God is present, and His people are present. United prayer includes a visible union (people gathered together) and an agreement of mind and heart. Agreeing together in prayer, however, is not just human agreement. God is involved. The kind of agreement we seek is agreeing with God in our requests. That kind of praying comes about only through the leadership of the Holy Spirit. When you agree with God in prayer, your request will be answered.

> ▶ **Read in the margin today's prayer promise, *Matthew 18:18-19*. Underline the promise God makes to you when you pray in agreement with others.**

Jesus promised that if we pray in agreement, our Father will do what we ask. In addition, Jesus taught us to pray,

> *'your will be done*
> *on earth as it is in heaven' (Matt. 6:10).*

When we pray in agreement, we seek His will to be done on earth. In a sense we pray in this sequence:
1. "Our Father in heaven, what is Your will in this matter?"
2. The Holy Spirit guides us to know the mind of the Father.
3. We pray: "Father, we ask You to do that on earth according to Your wishes. We agree with Your purposes and ways."

TODAY'S PRAYER PROMISE
"I tell you the truth, whatever you bind on earth will be bound in heaven, and whatever you loose on earth will be loosed in heaven.

"Again, I tell you that if two of you on earth agree about anything you ask for, it will be done for you by my Father in heaven" (Matt. 18:18-19).

4. God answers this prayer of agreement.

You may want to ask, "How can we get to the point at which we can hear and respond in prayer that way?" I believe that the following process is part of agreeing with God in prayer.

Get into agreement with God. As we have already studied this week, sin, unbelief, and wrong motives hinder our relationship with God. You cannot be in agreement with God when sin, unbelief, and wrong motives are present. The first step toward praying in agreement is to make right your relationship with God. All who are praying together must do the same. If one of you is wrong with the Lord, that broken relationship can hinder the whole group's prayer. Everyone must be right with the Lord to pray in agreement.

> *Pause to pray. Ask God to reveal any sin, unbelief, or wrong motives in your life that would hinder your relationship with Him. Pray for each member in your prayer group right now, asking God to help each person move to a right relationship with Him as well. Don't proceed until you have prayed.*

Get into agreement with others. The early church spent much time praying together with one mind and one heart: *They all joined together constantly in prayer (Acts 1:14). Every day they continued to meet together in the temple courts. They broke bread in their homes and ate together with glad and sincere hearts, praising God (Acts 2:46-47). All the believers were one in heart and mind. No one claimed that any of his possessions was his own, but they shared everything they had (Acts 4:32).* The church is a body, with every part dependent on the other parts. We need one another to function properly.

Sin and broken relationships can hinder our agreement with other believers. Jesus said: *"If you are offering your gift at the altar and there remember that your brother has something against you, leave your gift there in front of the altar. First go and be reconciled to your brother; then come and offer your gift." (Matt. 5:23-24).* Apply this same principle when you come to prayer. Until you are right with another person, you are not acceptable to the Lord. You cannot pray in agreement with another if anything is not right between you.

Many sins we studied in day 3 relate to others: anger, wrath, broken relationships, hypocrisy, indifference to need, iniquities (moral crookedness or failure), and unforgiveness. Pride is a major sin that may keep you from agreeing with others or from being reconciled with them. You must humble yourself and submit to one another to be of one heart and mind.

> *Pray and ask God to reveal to you any sin or broken relationship that you may have with other believers. If He reveals anything, begin the process of reconciliation.*

Seek God's perspective and pray in agreement with God. After you and all of the believers praying with you are right with God and with one another, you are ready to pray in agreement.

▶ Read "Suggestions for Praying Together" on page 93. Underline key ideas that will help you and your group pray in agreement.

Conclude your study by praying. Ask God to teach you and your prayer group how to pray in agreement. Ask Him to begin teaching you through your experience praying together this week.

Suggestions for Praying Together This Week

Be specific in what you ask of God. Ask the Holy Spirit to guide your praying according to God's will. Pay attention to the direction in which the Holy Spirit prompts you to pray. As you begin to form your request on a subject, check your spirit for confirmation of what others are praying. If a spirit of agreement prevails, express it. If a question or a doubt exists, express it. Don't hide questions or doubts from the Lord or those with whom you are praying. These questions may lead to further praying, which may lead to the correct request.

Consider God's viewpoint and give God reasons to answer. Consider these possible reasons: the prayer request can (1) uphold God's honor, (2) appeal for God's glory, (3) appeal to God's character, or (4) acknowledge God's sovereignty. Ask yourselves, *What would Jesus ask for?* Know that Jesus is praying with you and for you. Ask, "Holy Spirit, what do You want us to pray according to God's will?" Is this a request of a child to a Father or of a servant to a Master?

Use biblical principles, patterns, and promises to guide your requests. Pay attention to Scriptures that come to mind as you pray. They could be the Holy Spirit's promptings.

Seek Spirit-guided agreement with others in your prayers. Don't settle for mere human agreement. Pray on major issues until you come to one heart and mind on a matter. Listen to the prayers of others for direction or answers to your prayers. Often, guidance or direction comes while you are praying, not before. If heartfelt agreement does not come, keep on praying for days and weeks until God gives direction.

Week 5
Petition

This Week's Scripture-Memory Verse
"Ask and it will be given to you; seek and you will find; knock and the door will be opened to you" (Matt. 7:7).

This Week's Lessons
Day 1: Asking for Yourself
Day 2: A Model for Petition
Day 3: Following Your Father's Leading
Day 4: Praying for Yourself
Day 5: Asking Others to Pray for You

Summary of Week 5
Petition is asking for yourself, your family, your group, or your church. Your Heavenly Father leads your personal petition to mold you into the person He wants you to be. This week you will:
- learn that God invites personal petition;
- use biblical examples to identify the kinds of petition that God invites, hears, and answers;
- understand God's purpose in helping you become the kind of person He desires;
- realize the importance of asking others to pray for you;
- learn ways to be specific in praying for others.

This Week's Prayer Focus: Petition
God is your Heavenly Father. Through you He wants you to show the world what a child of God looks like. Therefore, He will guide your petitions. Through these prayers you will work with God as He helps you become more like Him.

This week focus on the following Scriptures of petition. Let your Heavenly Father guide your petitions as He works in your life.

Examples of Petition

"Give your servant a discerning heart to govern your people and to distinguish between right and wrong. For who is able to govern this great people of yours?" (1 Kings 3:9).

At the time of sacrifice, the prophet Elijah stepped forward and prayed: "O Lord, God of Abraham, Isaac and Israel, let it be known today that you are God in Israel and that I am your servant and have done all these things at your command. Answer me, O Lord, answer me, so these people will know that you, O Lord, are God, and that you are turning their hearts back again" (1 Kings 18:36-37).

"Oh, that you would bless me and enlarge my territory! Let your hand be with me, and keep me from harm" (1 Chron. 4:10).

"O Lord, let your ear be attentive to the prayer of this your servant and to the prayer of your servants who delight in revering your name. Give your servant success today by granting him favor in the presence of this man" (Neh. 1:11).

They were all trying to frighten us. . . . But I prayed, "Now strengthen my hands" (Neh. 6:9).

"My Father, if it is possible, may this cup be taken from me. Yet not as I will, but as you will" (Matt. 26:39).

"I do believe; help me overcome my unbelief!" (Mark 9:24).

Petitions from Psalms

Answer me when I call to you,
　　O my righteous God.
Give me relief from my distress;
　　be merciful to me and hear my prayer
　　　　　(Ps. 4:1).

O Lord, do not rebuke me in your anger
　　or discipline me in your wrath (Ps. 6:1).

O Lord my God, I take refuge in you;
　　save and deliver me from all who
　　　　　pursue me (Ps. 7:1).

To you, O Lord, I lift up my soul;
　　in you I trust, O my God.
Do not let me be put to shame,
　　nor let my enemies triumph over me
　　　　　(Ps. 25:1-2).

Hear my cry, O God;
　　listen to my prayer.
From the ends of the earth I call to you,
　　I call as my heart grows faint;
　　lead me to the rock that is higher
　　　　　than I (Ps. 61:1-2).

Hasten, O God, to save me;
　　O Lord, come quickly to help me
　　　　　(Ps. 70:1).

Teach me your way, O Lord,
　　and I will walk in your truth;
give me an undivided heart,
　　that I may fear your name (Ps. 86:11).

Search me, O God, and know my heart;
　　test me and know my anxious thoughts.
See if there is any offensive way in me,
　　and lead me in the way everlasting
　　　　　(Ps. 139:23-24).

Let the morning bring me word of your
　　　　　unfailing love,
　　for I have put my trust in you.
Show me the way I should go,
　　for to you I lift up my soul (Ps. 143:8).

Day 1
Asking for Yourself

SCRIPTURE-MEMORY VERSE
"Ask and it will be given to you; seek and you will find; knock and the door will be opened to you'"
(Matt. 7:7).

During these final two weeks you will study the asking prayers in more detail. This week's lessons will focus on petition; next week's, on intercession. Before we begin a detailed look at petition, review last week's lessons.

⚡ On page 50 read the Scriptures in the margin under "God Invites Asking."

On pages 51-52 read the eight reasons God answers prayer. Which three are most encouraging, meaningful, or helpful in your own praying? Write them below.

_____

_____

_____

Name four reasons God doesn't answer prayer. Review pages 53-54 if you need help.

_____   _____

_____   _____

On pages 55-56 read the nine principles for asking. Which two of these principles do you most need to work on to apply to your prayer life?

_____   _____

Of the following areas, which do you most need to work on to pray in agreement with God?
❑ Getting into agreement with God
❑ Getting into agreement with others
❑ Understanding God's desires for a particular request
❑ Praying with others long enough to agree together

Petition is asking for yourself, your family, your church, or your group. You might think that the great prayer warriors of the Bible did not emphasize personal petition. Yet many of them made personal petitions. In *Genesis 15:2* Abram (later Abraham) asked God for a son. In *1 Samuel 1:10-11* Hannah prayed for a son. King Hezekiah was dying and prayed to live (see *2 Kings 20:1-3*). Zechariah and Elizabeth prayed for a child (see *Luke 1:13*). God heard and answered all of these personal petitions.

► Based on these biblical examples, which of the following is true?
  ❏ Personal petition is selfish. God doesn't want us to pray for personal concerns.
  ❏ Personal petition is acceptable to the Lord since He answers and seems to encourage these personal requests.

The examples in the Bible indicate that God is pleased to hear your personal requests. God's purpose in encouraging petition is to mold you into a certain kind of person. In each example in the margin, the person praying was in the process of becoming a more godly person. Abraham didn't just receive a son; God gave him a nation. Hannah was becoming a certain kind of person when she prayed for a son, for motherhood changes the character of a woman of God. Hezekiah became one of Israel's greatest kings.

► What is a primary purpose in God's encouraging petition?

_____

In each case of personal petition above, not only the person but also God's work and kingdom benefited. Abraham's prayer resulted in the chosen race that would prepare the way for Christ. Hannah's prayer gave her son, Samuel, to Israel—a great judge and the first prophet. Because he did not die, Hezekiah lived to father Manasseh. In so doing, he preserved the messianic line of David that led to the birth of Jesus.

► Each biblical character we discussed illustrates the purpose of asking prayers. Can you recall that purpose?
  ❏ I identify with God by working with Him in His Kingdom.
  ❏ I identify with God by becoming like Him.

ABRAM
Abram said, "O Sovereign Lord, what can you give me since I remain childless and the one who will inherit my estate is Eliezer of Damascus?" (Gen. 15:2).

HANNAH
In bitterness of soul Hannah wept much and prayed to the Lord. And she made a vow, saying, 'O Lord Almighty, if you will only look upon your servant's misery and remember me, and not forget your servant but give her a son, then I will give him to the Lord for all the days of his life (1 Sam. 1:10-11).

HEZEKIAH
In those days Hezekiah became ill and was at the point of death. . . . Hezekiah turned his face to the wall and prayed to the Lord, "Remember, O Lord, how I have walked before you faithfully and with wholehearted devotion and have done what is good in your eyes." And Hezekiah wept bitterly (2 Kings 20:1-3).

ZECHARIAH
The angel said to him: "Do not be afraid, Zechariah; your prayer has been

heard. *Your wife Elizabeth will bear you a son, and you are to give him the name John" (Luke 1:13).*

Close today's study by thanking your Father for specific ways He has helped you become the person He wants you to be. Ask Him to continue showing you direction for your life. Begin to fix your thoughts on Jesus—your perfect example of godly living.

Day 2
A Model for Petition

TODAY'S PRAYER PROMISE
"He will call upon me, and I will answer him; I will be with him in trouble, I will deliver him and honor him" (Ps. 91:15).

Petition God for your personal needs. Jesus taught this practice to His disciples. In the Model Prayer, after the prayer for God's honor and Kingdom, Jesus authorized a series of personal requests.

Read the Model Prayer below. **Underline the three personal requests** in *verses 11-13.*

PROVERBS 30:7-9
"Two things I ask of you, O Lord; do not refuse me before I die: Keep false-hood and lies far from me; give me neither poverty nor riches, but give me only my daily bread. Otherwise, I may have too much and disown you and say, 'Who is the Lord?' Or I may become poor and steal, and so dishonor the name of my God."

> " 'Our Father in heaven,
> hallowed be your name,
> your kingdom come,
> your will be done
>   on earth as it is in heaven.
> Give us today our daily bread.
> Forgive us our debts,
>   as we also have forgiven our debtors.
> And lead us not into temptation,
> but deliver us from the evil one' " (Matt. 6:9-13).

Jesus taught us to pray for daily food, forgiveness of sins, and deliverance from temptation and the evil one. These represent three general areas in which God is interested:

- Your physical needs
- Restored fellowship with Him if you break it
- Protection from forces beyond your control

You are taught to pray for physical needs. You are not encouraged to pray for every *want*. In fact, too much material wealth can lead you away from God (see *Prov. 30:7-9*). God knows your needs and considers your motives (see *Jas. 4:3*). He makes no promises for selfish or greedy requests.

JAMES 4:3
When you ask, you do not receive, because you ask with wrong motives, that you may spend what you get on your pleasures.

God wants to have intimate fellowship with you. When you sin, the fellow-ship is broken. Confession of the sin begins the process of cultivating this fel-lowship. You must also seek His forgiveness and restoration.

Temptation (see *Matt. 6:13*) can refer to an enticement to sin or to a trial or testing. God promises that He will not allow you to be tested beyond what you can endure (see *1 Cor. 10:13* in the margin). He will offer you a way out. You can and should ask God for that deliverance.

Pause and pray these three requests for yourself: physical needs, restored fellowship with God, and protection from evil.

> Read in the margin the sample prayers of petition. Underline the petitions that would be meaningful for you to pray for yourself or for your group. Of those you underline, write one below that seems to be most needed now.

Ask for guidance. Jesus Himself practiced the principle of praying for personal needs. Jesus often prayed for guidance. The night before He chose the 12 disciples, Jesus spent the entire night in prayer (see *Luke 6:12-13*). When the time came to expand His ministry, Jesus arose early in the morning and prayed in *a solitary place* (see *Mark 1:35-39*). Jesus' prayers demonstrate that divine guidance is available through prayer.

> Do you have a specific need for God's guidance in an area of your life or work? Describe your need. Then pray for God's guidance.

_____

_____

Ask for wisdom. Another personal petition often found in Scripture is for wisdom. Asking for wisdom is appropriate: *If any of you lacks wisdom, he should ask God, who gives generously to all without finding fault, and it will be given to him (Jas. 1:5).*

Ask that His will be done. Personal requests should grow from a personal relationship with the Lord. Consider the way God views your personal requests. Think of two personal requests you have made recently or could make today. Prayerfully trace what would happen in the kingdom or for God's honor if those requests were granted. Learn to say, "Thy kingdom come in the granting of [specific personal request]." Be alert to ways your Father wants you to become a more godly person.

Close today's lesson with a time of personal petition.

1 CORINTHIANS 10:13
No temptation has seized you except what is common to man. And God is faithful; he will not let you be tempted beyond what you can bear. But when you are tempted, he will also provide a way out so that you can stand up under it.

SAMPLE PRAYERS OF PETITION
- Heavenly Father, I am Your child.
- Father, I want to be like You. I want to be like Jesus. Teach me to be [name desired characteristics].
- Fill me with Your Holy Spirit.
- Bring glory to Yourself in my body and my spirit
- Guide me to know the way I am to go.
- Lord, give me a spirit of wisdom, understanding, knowledge, and reverence for You.

Day 3
Following Your Father's Leading

You may not respond to a stranger who tries to sell you something over the telephone. But if you hear a friend's voice in the receiver, you will probably make time, even if your schedule is tight. Similarly, God answers prayer because of who you are in relation to Him.

After His resurrection Jesus told Mary Magdalene, *'I am returning to my Father and your Father, to my God and your God' (John 20:17).* Can you imagine Mary's feelings when Jesus included her in His family relationship with the Father? In the Model Prayer Jesus also commanded you to pray to God as Father (see *Matt. 6:9*). You are included, too! This relationship between you as a child and your Heavenly Father ought to influence the way you pray. You make your requests of a giving Father.

Read in the margin *James 1:17* and *Matthew 7:7-11.* What kind of gifts come down from the Father of heaven?

_____

Which of the following describes the kind of gifts God gives?
- ❑ God gives things that I don't ask for and that will harm me or fail to meet my needs.
- ❑ God gives good gifts that will meet my needs. He gives what I ask according to His will.

God is your Heavenly Father, who wants you to develop according to the plans He has for you. He cares what you become. He encourages personal petition to help you become the person He wants you to be. One day you will reign with Christ (see *Rev. 5:10*). God does not want you to be petty or immature. You are royalty and nobility! Your personal petitions should be directed by the Holy Spirit as He reveals the kind of person you are to become.

When you pray as a child to the Heavenly Father, you should emphasize growing spiritually. You may call Him Father as you talk to Him. Pray to become like Him and like Jesus. Pray for a life that represents the Father well. For His sake pray about maintaining your Father's reputation. Pray for ways to maintain the honor of the family name—Christian—and for characteristics God will develop in you.

⬇ Read *James 3:17* in the margin and underline the character traits (virtues) of godly wisdom. Read *Galatians 5:22-23* in the margin and underline the fruit of the Spirit. Read *Matthew 5:3-11* in the margin and underline attitudes the Lord blesses.

Here are some virtues God wants to develop in your life and attitudes He blesses. Pray for these traits.

CHRISTLIKE VIRTUES

Pure	Peace-loving	Considerate	Submissive
Merciful	Fruitful	Impartial	Sincere

FRUIT OF THE SPIRIT

Love	Joy	Peace	Patience	Kindness
Goodness	Faithfulness	Gentleness	Self-control	

BLESSED ATTITUDES

Poor in spirit—dependent on God	Merciful—forgiving, caring
Mourn—need the Comforter	Pure in heart—holy, clean
Meek—humble	Peacemaker—reconciler
Hunger for righteousness	Persecuted because of righteousness

Trust, a vital component of a family relationship, is a basis for prayer. On one occasion when some of the Israelites were facing an enemy in battle, *They were helped in fighting them, . . . because they cried out to him during the battle. He answered their prayers, because they trusted in him (1 Chron. 5:20).* You can trust your Father's leading. What He leads you to become will always be best.

Pause and pray through the lists of virtues and attitudes you studied today. Ask God to work in you to develop these characteristics. Allow Him to do whatever is necessary to make you the person He wants you to be. The result will always be worth the cost!

REVELATION 5:10
" 'You have made them to be a kingdom and priests to serve our God, and they will reign on the earth.' "

JAMES 3:17
The wisdom that comes from heaven is first of all pure; then peace-loving, considerate, submissive, full of mercy and good fruit, impartial and sincere.

GALATIANS 5:22-23
The fruit of the Spirit is love, joy, peace, patience, kindness, goodness, faithfulness, gentleness and self-control. Against such things there is no law.

MATTHEW 5:3-11
"Blessed are the poor in spirit. . . .
Blessed are those who mourn. . .
Blessed are the meek. . . .
Blessed are those who hunger and thirst for righteousness. . . .
Blessed are the merciful. . . .
Blessed are the pure in heart. . . .
Blessed are the peacemakers. . . .
Blessed are those who are persecuted because of righteousness."

Day 4
Praying for Yourself

TODAY'S PRAYER PROMISE
"Whatever you ask for in prayer, believe that you have received it, and it will be yours" (Mark 11:24).

as you learned last week, you can use prayer lists to help you remember to pray for specific concerns. Today you will prepare lists for personal petition.

Prepare lists of personal needs or concerns for which you wish to pray. Use the following categories to stimulate your thinking. Ask your Heavenly Father to guide your requests according to His will and purposes for His Kingdom and your life.

Virtues or attitudes God wants to develop in me: _____

_____

Spiritual needs to be restored to fellowship with my Father: _____

_____

Spiritual needs to be reconciled with fellow Christians: _____

List needs or concerns for which you wish to pray.

_____

Spiritual growth and maturity: _____

_____

Being a godly family member: _____

_____

Being a faithful church member: _____

_____

Guidance for family, school, church, and ministry: _____

_____

Strength to overcome temptations: _____

_____

Deliverance or protection: _____

_____

Enabling for spiritual ministry: _____

_____

A powerful and bold witness: _____

_____

Emotional needs or concerns: _____

_____

Ask your Heavenly Father to guide your requests according to His will and purposes.

Material or financial needs: _____

_____

Health-and-fitness needs: _____

_____

Others: _____

_____

_____

_____

Take time to pray for some of these requests. Emphasize spiritual concerns in your prayers. If you first seek God's kingdom, many of your needs will also be met. Don't hesitate, however, to pray for your human needs. Your Father also cares about them.

Day 5
Asking Others to Pray for You

Paul asked the churches of his time to pray with him and for him.

⚡ Read the Scriptures in the margin. Underline subjects for which Paul wanted others to pray in his behalf.

You might ask: Why should I ask someone else to pray for me? Doesn't God hear my prayers? God wants you to ask others to pray for you, and we have biblical reasons to do so. Paul, for example, was convinced that the prayers of other Christians would strengthen his own prayers.

⚡ Read the following reasons to ask others to pray for you. Circle the numbers beside the ones that seem most meaningful to you. Ask God to show you why you need the prayers of others.

Asking Others to Pray for You

1. *Shows your dependence on God.* God will do some things only in answer to prayer. This way you know that God is the One who provided or acted, and He receives the glory for His actions.
2. *Demonstrates lowliness before God and humility before others.* Pride keeps you from asking others to pray for you.

> Clothe yourselves with humility toward one another, because,
> "God opposes the proud
> but gives grace to the humble."
> Humble yourselves, therefore, under God's mighty hand, that he
> may lift you up in due time. Cast all your anxiety on him because he
> cares for you (1 Pet. 5:5-7).

3. *Brings greater authority to prayer.* God grants greater authority to united prayers of agreement: *"If two of you on earth agree about anything you ask for, it will be done for you by my Father in heaven" (Matt.18:19).*
4. *Increases the amount of praying in your behalf.* The more persons who pray, the more petition is made in your behalf.
5. *Broadens the understanding of how to pray for your need.* Others may

ROMANS 15:30
"I urge you, brothers, by our Lord Jesus Christ and by the love of the Spirit, to join me in my struggle by praying to God for me."

EPHESIANS 6:19
"Pray also for me, that whenever I open my mouth, words may be given me so that I will fearlessly make known the mystery of the gospel."

1 THESSALONIANS 5:25
"Pray for us."

2 THESSALONIANS 3:1
"Pray for us that the message of the Lord may spread rapidly and be honored, just as it was with you."

know exactly how to pray for you even when you don't. They may have been through the same experience. Their specific prayers may secure God's answer for your need.

6. *Blesses those who have the privilege of praying for you.* When people pray for you, they receive a blessing. It is multiplied when they learn that God has answered their prayers. Be sure to give reports of answered prayer to those who pray for you.

7. *Strengthens the bond of love between you and those who pray for you.* When a person begins to pray intently for another, a bond of love is created or strengthened.

8. *Secures strength for an area of personal weakness or failure.*

When You Pray for Others

One need in praying together is praying specific and meaningful prayers. To help focus your prayers, put yourself in the place of the one for whom you are praying so that you can "feel" what she feels. What feelings is she dealing with? Think of problems, conflicts, or pressures the person may face.

Put yourself in the place of the one for whom you are praying.

If you pray for a friend who is grieving over the loss of a family member, for example, think about the issues he must deal with. You might pray feelings of loneliness, anger, and bitterness. You might continue praying about changes the grieving person might confront, like facing holidays. When you put yourself in his circumstances, you can pray much more specifically—especially if you have faced similar circumstances.

▶ Think about the members of your prayer group and personal concerns they have shared in past weeks. Does one person stand out as someone for whom God wants you to pray? Choose one and write his or her name here:

_____

Try to put yourself in the person's place. List in the margin concerns for which you can pray in this person's behalf.

You may want to pay attention to specific ways you can be part of the answer to your prayers. As you pray, God may give you a burden to help meet a need. Listen for directions God may give you for meeting the person's needs. These often come only during prayer.

Close your study today by praying for the person you have chosen. Pray specifically for the needs or concerns you have listed. Ask the Holy Spirit to guide your praying in areas you may not have considered.

Suggestions for Praying Together This Week

As you pray together, listen carefully for opportunities to respond to others' prayers. If a person makes a personal petition in prayer, you might intercede for that need or concern. If a person prays for forgiveness, you might ask the Lord for forgiveness, cleansing, and restoration. If a person asks the Lord a question, be sensitive to the fact that God may speak the answer through you. One person's intercession may spark a thought about how you are to pray. As you learn to pray together, you will find that God often uses someone's prayer to guide you in what to pray next.

When a person's prayer causes a Scripture to come to mind, pay attention to what God may be saying through that Scripture. If your spirit agrees with what someone is praying, then tell the Lord that you agree. These kinds of prayers will greatly increase your faith as you pray. God can and will guide you to pray in a specific direction so that you know that the answer has been granted. Then you can wait in great expectation for the answer.

God often uses someone's prayer to guide you in what to pray next.

Week 6

Intercession

This Week's Scripture Memory Verse

Confess your sins to each other and pray for each other so that you may be healed. The prayer of a righteous man is powerful and effective (Jas. 5:16).

This Week's Lessons

Day 1: Asking for Others
Day 2: Examples of Intercession
Day 3: Following Your Master's Leading
Day 4: Praying for Others
Day 5: Praying Together in God's Work

Summary of Week 6

Intercession is asking for others that is led by your Master. This week you will:

- understand your relationship as a servant to God, your Master;
- learn how to join God's work by seeking and praying for His desires;
- understand why intercession is the greater kind of asking and why a call to intercession is one of God's highest callings for a person's life;
- follow biblical models of intercession to pray more effectively for others;
- understand how God works through united prayer to reveal His will and purpose to a church or a group;
- discuss what your group will do after this study has ended.

This Week's Prayer Focus: Intercession

God is Master, and you are His Servant. He is working in the world to reconcile the lost to Himself through Christ. In carrying out kingdom purposes, God has chosen you to labor with Him. One way to work with God is through prayers of intercession. Intercessory prayers are for God's kingdom purposes to be completed in the lives of others. Your Master will lead your prayers according to His purposes.

This week focus on the following Scriptures of intercession. Let your Master guide your praying according to His kingdom purposes. Labor together with God in your prayers of intercession. Praise, worship, and thank Him for every answer He allows you to see.

Examples of Intercession

"O Lord, open his eyes so he may see." Then the Lord opened the servant's eyes, and he looked and saw the hills full of horses and chariots of fire all around Elisha (2 Kings 6:17).

"O Lord, God of our fathers Abraham, Isaac and Israel, keep this desire in the hearts of your people forever, and keep their hearts loyal to you" (1 Chron. 29:18).

"Holy Father, protect them by the power of your name—the name you gave me—so that they may be one as we are one. My prayer is not that you take them out of the world but that you protect them from the evil one. . . . Sanctify them by the truth; your word is truth. . . . I pray also for those who will believe in me through their message, that all of them may be one, Father, just as you are in me and I am in you. May they also be in us so that the world may believe that you have sent me. . . . that they may be one as we are one: I in them and you in me. May they be brought to complete unity to let the world know that you sent me and have loved them even as you have loved me" (John 17:11,15,17,20-23).

Paul's Example

Brothers, my heart's desire and prayer to God for the Israelites is that they be saved (Rom. 10:1).

I pray that out of his glorious riches he may strengthen you with power through his Spirit in your inner being, so that Christ may dwell in your hearts through faith. And I pray that you, being rooted and established in love, may have power, together with all the saints, to grasp how wide and long and high and deep is the love of Christ, and to know this love that surpasses knowledge—that you may be filled to the measure of all the fullness of God (Eph. 3:16-19).

We have not stopped praying for you and asking God to fill you with the knowledge of his will through all spiritual wisdom and understanding. And we pray this in order that you may live a life worthy of the Lord and may please him in every way: bearing fruit in every good work, growing in the knowledge of God, being strengthened with all power according to his glorious might so that you may have great endurance and patience, and joyfully giving thanks to the Father, who has qualified you to share in the inheritance of the saints in the kingdom of light (Col. 1:9-12).

Jesus' Example

Jesus went out to a mountainside to pray, and spent the night praying to God. When morning came, he called his disciples to him and chose twelve of them, whom he also designated apostles (Luke 6:12-13).

Stephen's Example

He fell on his knees and cried out, "Lord, do not hold this sin against them." When he had said this, he fell asleep (Acts 7:60).

A Church's Example

Peter was kept in prison, but the church was earnestly praying to God for him (Acts 12:5).

Epaphras's Example

Epaphras . . . is always wrestling in prayer for you, that you may stand firm in all the will of God, mature and fully assured (Col. 4:12).

Day 1
Asking for Others

Petition is asking for yourself, your family, or your church. Petition is led by your Heavenly Father. A second kind of asking prayer is intercession. Intercession is asking for others that is led by your Master.

▶ **What is the second kind of asking prayer?**

1. Petition

2._____

God is your Master. You are His servant. God is working to reconcile a lost world to Himself through Christ. He is carrying out His kingdom purposes and has chosen you to be His servant to labor with Him in the kingdom. One way to work with God is through prayers of intercession—praying for others and praying for kingdom purposes to be completed in their lives. God, as your Master, will lead your prayers according to His purposes.

▶ **Who leads prayers of intercession?**

My_____

An Example of Jesus' Intercession
Jesus prayed for His disciples. At the Last Supper Jesus told the disciples that Satan had asked permission to sift them like wheat. Jesus then told Simon: *"I have prayed for you, Simon, that your faith may not fail. And when you have turned back, strengthen your brothers"* (Luke 22:32). This prayer made possible Peter's great courage before the Sanhedrin: *"When they [the Sanhedrin] saw the courage of Peter and John and realized that they were unschooled, ordinary men, they were astonished and they took note that these men had been with Jesus"* (Acts 4:13; also see *vv. 8-12*). Intercessory prayer reaches its highest potential when it is intended to further the kingdom of God and to accomplish His will.

The Greater Kind of Asking
Years ago I began to study all of the prayers of the Bible, especially the asking prayers that were answered with a yes. Eighty of the answered asking prayers in the Bible were personal petition. One hundred thirty-one were intercession.

SCRIPTURE-MEMORY VERSE
"Confess your sins to each other and pray for each other so that you may be healed. The prayer of a righteous man is powerful and effective" (Jas. 5:16).

Intercessory prayer reaches its highest potential when it is intended to further the kingdom of God and to accomplish His will.

All of God's servants are called to be intercessors.

Intercession is the more important kind of asking.

All of God's servants are called to be intercessors. Some seem to receive a more specific calling to intense intercession. We often call these persons prayer warriors—persons who wage spiritual battles in intercessory prayer. The calling to be an intercessor is a high calling.

☑ Have you ever sensed God's calling to a deeper-than-usual role of intercessory prayer? ☐ Yes ☐ No If you answered yes, briefly describe your sense of calling and how you have responded.

_____

_____

ROMANS 8:34
Christ Jesus . . . is at the right hand of God and is also interceding for us.

HEBREWS 7:25
He [Jesus] is able to save completely those who come to God through him, because he always lives to intercede for them.

Read in the margin *Romans 8:34* and *Hebrews 7:25*. Which two persons of the Trinity intercede for you?

_____ and _____

Jesus and the Holy Spirit are intercessors. When God calls you to be an intercessor, you join Jesus and the Holy Spirit in their work. That is a high calling indeed.

☑ How would you rate the importance of being an intercessor?
   ☐ Not very important. Other work is far more important.
   ☐ It may be important but only in a crisis.
   ☐ Very important—it is also the job of Jesus and the Holy Spirit.

The biblical pattern is that God often did His work through the prayers of great intercessors. When God wanted to deliver the children of Israel from bondage, he raised up Moses to pray for them. When He wanted to deliver them from the murderous plot of Haman, He raised up Esther to fast for them. To rebuild the Jerusalem wall and to renew the covenant, God used the prayers of Nehemiah and Ezra. He started the missionary movement through the prayers of the church in Antioch. The biblical pattern tells us that God does not usually work by Himself. He prefers to work through the prayers of His saints. Intercession is God's basic method for accomplishing His will among people.

Intercession is God's basic method for accomplishing His will among people.

Ask God to train you to be an intercessor. Offer your life to Him for any job of intercession to which He may call you.

Day 2
Examples of Intercession

Intercessory prayer is so important that it can make the difference between life and death. During the early days of the church King Herod put James to death. Because this pleased the Jews, Herod arrested Peter with the plan to kill him also. *Peter was kept in prison, but the church was earnestly praying to God for him (Acts 12:5).* In the night an angel of the Lord delivered Peter from prison. Peter immediately went to the house of Mary and John Mark, *where many people had gathered and were praying (Acts 12:12).* God worked through the prayers of the early church to spare Peter's life for further service. Your prayers and the prayers of your group could have similar importance in God's kingdom.

Turn back to pages 73-74 and read other examples of intercession.

Who prayed all night? _____

Who wrestled in prayer for God's people? _____

Who prayed for God to forgive those who were killing him?

_____

What are some of the things Paul prayed for churches?

_____

_____

_____

_____

_____

Jesus, Epaphras, and Stephen were intercessors. Paul was also a great intercessor who earnestly prayed for churches. Some of the things for which He prayed are listed in the margin.

TODAY'S PRAYER PROMISE
"If my people, who are called by my name, will humble themselves and pray and seek my face and turn from their wicked ways, then will I hear from heaven and will forgive their sin and will heal their land" (2 Chron. 7:14).

PAUL'S PRAYERS FOR CHURCHES
- Knowledge of God's will, spiritual wisdom, and understanding
- Worthy living that would please the Lord
- Spiritual fruit bearing
- Growth in the knowledge of God
- Strength and power
- Endurance, patience, and joy
- Faith, love, and spiritual fullness

JOHN 17:11-12,15-23
11" 'Holy Father, protect them by the power of your name—the name you gave me—so that they may be one as we are one. 12While I was with them, I protected them and **kept**

them safe by that name you gave me.

¹⁵"My prayer is not that you take them out of the world but that you protect them from the evil one. ¹⁶They are not of the world, even as I am not of it. ¹⁷Sanctify them by the truth; your word is truth. ¹⁸As you sent me into the world, I have sent them into the world. ¹⁹For them I sanctify myself, that they too may be truly sanctified.

²⁰"My prayer is not for them alone. I pray also for those who will believe in me through their message, ²¹that all of them may be one, Father, just as you are in me and I am in you. May they also be in us so that the world may believe that you have sent me. ²²I have given them the glory that you gave me, that they may be one as we are one: ²³I in them and you in me. May they be brought to complete unity to let the world know that you sent me and have loved them even as you have loved me."

Stop and pray the following requests for your church. Which request is your greatest burden for God to grant? Why?

- *Knowledge of God's will, spiritual wisdom, and understanding*
- *Worthy living that would please the Lord*
- *Spiritual fruit bearing*
- *Growth in the knowledge of God*
- *Strength and power*
- *Endurance, patience, and joy*
- *Faith, love, and spiritual fullness*

The Bible has many examples of intercessory prayer. You can learn from these examples. Let's examine Jesus' great intercessory prayer in *John 17*. Concerned about His followers, Jesus prayed for His disciples' spiritual needs. He prayed for them because these would be the leaders in promoting the kingdom of God. For His disciples Jesus requested unity, protection and deliverance, and sanctification or holiness.

Read in the margin the verses from *John 17*. On the lines write the verse numbers that relate to each prayer request.

Unity: _____ Protection and deliverance: _____

Sanctification or holiness: _____

Jesus prayed that His disciples might be one. The great unity He wanted had been disturbed by a quarrel among the disciples about who would be the greatest (see *Luke 22:24-27*). Jesus asked for that unity four times from four perspectives. He and the disciples had the same power *(v. 11)*, relationship to the Father *(v. 21)*, witness to the world *(v. 23)*, and name *(vv. 11-12)*. Because unity was so significant to Jesus, it ought to be part of your prayers, too. Pray for unity not just for one local congregation or one denomination but for all who belong to God through faith in His Son, Jesus.

Jesus also prayed for the disciples' protection, deliverance, and sanctification. *Sanctified* means *made holy*, and *holy* means *set apart*. No impurity from the world should be allowed into the hearts of God's people, who have been set apart for His work.

Pray these prayers for your church: for unity, protection, deliverance, and sanctification (being set apart, holy, pure). Write in the margin any specific ways you feel led to pray for your church.

Day 3
Following Your Master's Leading

When Jesus began His earthly ministry, He preached this message: *"Repent, for the kingdom of heaven is near" (Matt. 4:17).* Jesus is the King of this kingdom. The kingdom Jesus spoke of is His rule in the hearts of His people. He is the King, and we are His subjects. He is the Master, and we are His servants (see *1 Cor. 7:22-23*). When you trusted Christ as your Savior, He also became Lord (Master) of your life. As a servant of God, you have tasks to complete that represent His work.

> Beside each word indicate whether the role belongs to Christ or to you. Write either a *C* for *Christ* or an *m* for *me*.
> _____ Servant   _____ Master   _____ Subject
> _____ King   _____ Lord

Jesus is King, Master, and Lord. You are servant and subject. A servant never tells the Master what to do. The Master decides what is important. As God's servant, you join Him in the work He is doing. This was Jesus' approach in knowing and doing His Father's will (see *John 5:17,19-20*). When you pray as a servant, the emphasis is on God's work. Your objects in prayer are to know the mind and heart of your Master and to pray for His kingdom to come and His will to be done.

> Where should your prayer requests originate as you pray for God's kingdom to come and His will to be done?
> ❑ I do my best thinking and decide what to ask God to do.
> ❑ I seek God's direction for my prayer requests.

As your Master, God will lead your intercession. As you pray for others or for kingdom purposes, seek God's direction for your prayer requests. This may seem strange to you if you have not experienced God's directing your prayers. God is able to give you direction if you are willing to seek it and to wait on Him for an answer.

Servanthood secures God's interest in your prayers for His work. Through the power and authority of the prayers He leads you to pray, God accomplishes His work. Intercession begins and ends in God.

When you pray, you may call Jesus your Master. This will help you keep in mind that He is the One who directs the work of intercession. On the Lord's

TODAY'S PRAYER PROMISE
The Spirit helps us in our weakness. We do not know what we ought to pray for, but the Spirit himself intercedes for us with groans that words cannot express. And he who searches our hearts knows the mind of the Spirit, because the Spirit intercedes for the saints in accordance with God's will (Rom. 8:26-27).

1 CORINTHIANS 7:22-23
He who was a slave when he was called by the Lord is the Lord's freedman; similarly, he who was a free man when he was called is Christ's slave. You were bought at a price; do not become slaves of men.

Intercession begins and ends in God.

"Ask the Lord of the harvest, therefore, to send out workers into his harvest field" (Matt. 9:38).

Pray in the Spirit on all occasions with all kinds of prayers and requests. With this in mind, be alert and always keep on praying for all the saints (Eph. 6:18).

I urge, then, first of all, that requests, prayers, intercession and thanksgiving be made for everyone— for kings and all those in authority, that we may live peaceful and quiet lives in all godliness and holiness (1 Tim. 2:1-2).

Confess your sins to each other and pray for each other so that you may be healed. The prayer of a righteous man is powerful and effective (Jas. 5:16).

"Love your enemies and pray for those who persecute you" (Matt. 5:44).

---

behalf, pray for the spread of His kingdom and for right relationships with other servants. Pray that His blessings and works will demonstrate His lordship and righteousness.

Your Master will guide your praying according to His will. He has revealed in His Word some of the topics for which He wants you to pray.

◩ **Read the verses in the margins. Below each Scripture write the name of someone for whom you can pray.**

The Bible also describes your Master's concerns. As you read and study the Scriptures, you will learn subjects about which to pray. When you read, *The Lord . . . is patient with you, not wanting anyone to perish, but everyone to come to repentance (2 Pet. 3:9)*, you can pray for God's continued patience and for the salvation of the lost.

Micah 6:8 says,

> *What does the Lord require of you?*
> *To act justly and to love mercy*
> *and to walk humbly with your God.*

Thus, you can pray for justice, mercy, and humility.

In *Isaiah 58:6-7* God reveals actions that please Him:

> *"Is not this the kind of fasting I have chosen:*
> *to loose the chains of injustice . . .*
> *to set the oppressed free . . .*
> *to share your food with the hungry*
> *   and to provide the poor wanderer with shelter—*
> *when you see the naked, to clothe him,*
> *   and not to turn away from your own flesh and blood?"*

Approach your Master in prayer. Ask Him to reveal His purposes and to guide your intercession for others. Pray for the persons and concerns described in today's lesson. Work together with Him as you pray for His kingdom to come and His will to be done on earth as it is in heaven.

Day 4
Praying for Others

nstead of learning more about prayer today, you will spend time praying for others. As you learned in week 4, you can use prayer lists to help you remember to pray for specific persons and concerns.

List below persons for whom you need to pray. Ask God to bring to mind persons for whom He wants you to intercede.

Your family members

_____   _____

_____   _____

Members of your church family:

_____   _____

_____   _____

Your pastor and other church leaders:

_____   _____

_____   _____

Relatives, friends, and acquaintances:

_____   _____

_____   _____

Other churches and denominations:

_____   _____

_____   _____

TODAY'S PRAYER PROMISE
Now to him who is able to do immeasurably more than all we ask or imagine, according to his power that is at work within us, to him be glory in the church and in Christ Jesus throughout all generations, for ever and ever! Amen. (Eph. 3:20-21).

Ask God to bring to mind persons for whom He wants you to intercede.

Possible Requests
- **Assurance**
- **Bold witnessing**
- **Calling of Christian workers**
- **Christian fruit**
- **Conviction of sin**
- **Deliverance**
- **Endurance**
- **Faith**
- **Faithfulness**
- **Filling of the Holy Spirit**
- **Forgiveness**
- **Generosity**
- **Guidance, God's will**

- Healing—spiritual, emotional, physical
- Holiness
- Hope
- Humility
- Integrity
- Joy
- Judgment
- Justice
- Knowledge
- Love
- Loyalty
- Mercy
- Obedience
- Patience
- Peace
- Preservation
- Provision of needs
- Purity
- Reconciliation of broken relationships
- Repentance and revival among God's people
- Right conduct
- Right motives
- Spirit of servanthood
- Spiritual awakening and conversion of the lost
- Spiritual cleansing
- Spiritual growth
- Stewardship
- Surrender and submission
- Understanding
- Wisdom

Missionaries (home and foreign):

_____   _____

_____   _____

Ministry leaders:

_____   _____

_____   _____

Civil authorities (local, regional, and national):

_____   _____

_____   _____

Your city, state, province, and nation:

_____   _____

_____   _____

Needy or poor persons:

_____   _____

_____   _____

Oppressed, abused, or victimized persons:

_____   _____

_____   _____

Hungry and homeless persons:

_____   _____

_____   _____

Widows, orphans, and prisoners:

_____   _____

_____   _____

Sick and homebound persons:

_____   _____

_____   _____

Your enemies—those who persecute you:

_____   _____

_____   _____

Take time to pray for these persons. In the margins on the previous pages you will find items you may want to request of the Lord. Be specific in your prayers.

Day 5
Praying Together in God's Work

Your church is the body of Christ. Christ is its Head, and every believer is a member of the body. Each member has a function in the body. Think about your physical body for a moment. What would you miss if you had no sight, hearing, smell, touch, or taste? Missing any one of your senses would prevent your body from knowing all it can of the physical world.

In a similar way, all of the members of the body are needed to function where God put them in your church body. If some members are not functioning, your church body is limited in knowing all it can of the spiritual world. As you pray about God's will and purposes, you cannot know God's will for the body without the participation of the other members of your spiritual body. Every contribution adds to your understanding of God's will and of how to pray accordingly.

Think of God's will for your church as a jigsaw puzzle. God gives each member one piece. By itself your piece may not make sense. But as each piece is

TODAY'S PRAYER PROMISE
I urge, then, first of all, that requests, prayers, intercession and thanksgiving be made for everyone—for kings and all those in authority, that we may live peaceful and quiet lives in all godliness and holiness. This is good, and pleases God our Savior, who wants all men to be saved and to come to a knowledge of the truth (1 Tim. 2:1-4).

shared with the body and put into its place, a beautiful picture begins to become clear. This is why your church needs to share and pray together.

My understanding of God's Will/Purposes

_____
_____
_____
_____
_____
_____

My Prayer Group's Understanding of God's Will/Purposes

_____
_____
_____
_____
_____
_____

My Church's Understanding of God's Will/Purposes

_____
_____
_____
_____
_____
_____

Think about your part of the jigsaw puzzle, which represents God's work for your church. In the margin list things you sense God wants to do in or through your church. This is not a brainstorming session for you to list your ideas. Rather, you need to identify what God has been saying to you. If something comes to mind as you pray through this activity, write it down. As you share these ideas with others, God will either confirm them or not confirm them. Trust that He can and will. Thank Him either way and don't feel offended if an item is not confirmed. All you want is to know your Master's will. Now pray; then consider the following questions as you make your list.

- What burdens has God given you as you have prayed about His will and about your place in His will for your church?
- What needs in your community have you felt a God-given burden to meet?
- What activity in and around your church may indicate an invitation for you to join God's work?
- What scriptural command(s) has God used to convict you about an area your church needs to address (for example, ministry to the poor, needy, oppressed, widows and orphans, or ministries of tithing, loving, witnessing, teaching, and discipling)?
- Might the kinds of members God has been adding to your body indicate God's preparation for an assignment (for example, medical personnel for medical-missions work, ethnic persons for starting a new church, or construction personnel for building churches in missions areas)?

Have you listed things that you sense God may want to do through your church or prayer group? This may be your part of the message God wants to reveal to your church or group about His will. In your prayer session this week you will have an opportunity to share items on your list. Others will share their lists. Then together you will seek God's perspective on areas He may want you to pray about more completely. This may be a very exciting time as you pray together about God's work in and through your church or group. You may find that God will speak clearly during the prayer time about something special of which He is calling you to be a part.

The early church in the New Testament prayed together about many concerns related to God's will and purposes. They prayed for boldness in witnessing, Christian fruit, the filling of the Spirit, conduct worthy of the Lord, spiritual enlightenment and understanding, deliverance from evil or preservation, the sick, church leaders, missionaries, and persons in authority.

Begin praying now for your group prayer time. Ask God to guide your praying according to His will and purposes. Ask Him to speak clearly to your prayer group and to your church about His will and purposes. Don't forget to pray for the larger body of Christ—other churches, denominations, missionaries and believers in other states, provinces, or countries—that God's kingdom will come and His will be done on earth as it is in heaven.

Guidelines for Group Prayer Sessions

Each week this section will guide your group to spend time together in prayer. Although each session is planned for one hour, do not let this guide restrict your praying. Freely follow the Holy Spirit's leadership. You may want to enlist a person or several persons to facilitate your prayer times.

*If my people,
who are called by my name,
will humble themselves and pray
and seek my face
and turn from their wicked ways,
then will I hear from heaven
and will forgive their sin
and will heal their land.*

2 Chronicles 7:14

Session 1
Six Kinds of Prayer

Preparing to Pray (15 minutes)

1. Review "Suggestions for Praying Together" on page 93. Remind members of suggestions from the previous session for praying together more effectively.
2. *Confession.* Ask members to spend time praying privately to prepare themselves to enter this prayer time. Encourage them to confess any known sins and to seek the Lord's cleansing.

Prayer Time (40 minutes)

1. Begin by acknowledging God's presence. Ask Him to guide your praying and to teach you to pray together effectively.
2. *Praise.* Invite group members to focus attention on God's attributes. Spend time praising God for who He is. You may want someone to read the attributes listed on page 39. Consider singing or reading a hymn of praise.
3. *Worship.* Encourage members to express to God their reverence, honor, adoration, and love. They should tell God why they love Him.
4. *Thanksgiving.* Thank God for His grace, His riches, and His blessings. Be specific, focusing especially on spiritual blessings. Consider personal, family, church, and other areas in which God has worked. Do not rush this segment.
5. *Petition and Intercession.* Remind members to share their prayer requests as they pray. Focus on one subject at a time. Encourage members to pray as often as they want. Allow members to introduce requests during your praying. Do not hesitate to pray for specific individuals. Consider praying for these subjects as time permits:
   - Your church: for unity, purity, boldness, and faithfulness.
   - Your pastor, church staff, and their families
   - Your prayer group and the following weeks of study and united prayer
   - Spiritual leaders in your denomination and in your nation
   - National and local governmental leaders
   - Home and foreign missions and missionaries
   - Revival and reconciliation among God's people, churches, and denominations
   - Spiritual awakening in the nation, through which lost persons come to Christ in large numbers
6. Close the prayer time as you feel led.

Reflection (5 minutes)

Explain that the purpose of the reflection time is not to criticize others but to help one another learn more effective ways to pray together. As a group, use the questions on pages 93-94 to assess the effectiveness of your prayer time. Record any suggestions for improving the next session. Because you will use this list to reflect on each prayer session, you may wish to list the questions on poster board for display at the end of each prayer session.

Encourage members to memorize the suggested Scripture-memory verse each week of the study.

Session 2
Developing Your Prayer Life

Preparing to pray (5 minutes)

See "Preparing to Pray" for Session 1 at the top of this page.

Prayer Time (50 minutes)

1. *Confession.* Acknowledge God's presence and

participation in your prayer time. Ask members to confess truths about God and their relationships with Him.

2. *Praise.* Turn to pages 21-22 and take turns praying aloud the examples of praise from the Scriptures. Using these as examples, voice your own prayers of praise to the Lord.

3. *Worship.* Turn to pages 34-35 and take turns praying aloud the examples of worship from the Scriptures. Using these as examples, voice your own prayers of worship to the Lord.

4. *Thanksgiving.* Ask members to pray one-sentence prayers of thanksgiving to the Lord. They may pray several times. Remind them to include thanking the Lord for spiritual blessings.

5. *Petition.* Ask members to pray in specific ways that God will help your church become a house of prayer. Spend as much time on this request as God seems to guide.

6. *Intercession.* Ask members to share prayer requests as they pray. Encourage others to join in prayer for each subject. Continue this period of intercession as long as time permits.

7. *Closure.* Close by reciting in unison the Model Prayer *(Matt. 6:9-13; see margin, p. 31).*

Reflection (5 minutes)

As a group, use the questions on page 94 to assess the effectiveness of your prayer time. Record any suggestions for improving the next session.

Encourage members to begin using lists to organize and guide their praying.

Session 3
Responding Prayers

Because this week's prayer session focuses on responding prayers, plan to spend extra time in confession, praise, worship, and thanksgiving. Use these suggestions only as a guide. As you develop confidence praying together, you may wish to depend less on these suggestions, allowing the Holy Spirit to direct your prayer time.

Preparing to Pray (5 minutes)

See "Preparing to Pray" for session 1 on page 87

Prayer Time (50 minutes)

1. *Confession.* Acknowledge God's presence. Ask members to confess truths about God and their relationships with Him. Use these other subjects for confession:
   • Confess sins to one another, following the guidelines on page 45.
   • Confess your needs, the needs of others, and the needs of your church.
   • Confess your new nature in Christ. Agree with God about the person you are becoming.
   • Confess Jesus as Savior and Lord.
   • Confess the rightness of God's ways.

2. *Praise.* Invite group members to praise God for who He is. Ask members to make statements of praise to God, focusing on one or more attributes. They may want to read Scriptures of praise or to quote a line of praise from a hymn. After each statement of praise ask members to quote together these phrases from *Psalm 67:3: Let the people praise thee, O God; let all the people praise thee* (KJV).

3. *Worship.* Ask several members to turn to pages 34-35 and to read one Scripture each as a prayer to the Lord in worship. Then encourage members to express to God their reverence, honor, and adoration, and love. They should tell God why they love Him.

4. *Thanksgiving.* Instruct members to thank God for the spiritual riches with which He has blessed them: redemption, forgiveness, adoption, a call to ministry, and the Holy Spirit. Thank Him for friends and relationships, health, home, and material blessings. Encourage members to be specific.

5. *Petition and intercession.* Remind members to share their prayer requests as they pray. Focus on one subject at a time. Encourage members to pray as often as they want. Allow them to make requests during the praying. Do not hesitate to pray for specific individuals. Consider praying for these subjects as time permits:

- Your church: for unity, purity, boldness, faithfulness
- Your pastor, church staff, and their families
- Your prayer group and the following weeks of study and united prayer
- Spiritual leaders in your denomination and in your nation
- National and local governmental leaders
- Home and foreign missions and missionaries
- Revival and reconciliation among God's people, churches, and denominations
- Spiritual awakening in the nation, through which lost persons come to Christ in large numbers

6. Invite members to join hands. Call on one person to read the following benediction from *Jude 24-25:*
To him who is able to keep you from falling and to present you before his glorious presence without fault and with great joy—to the only God our Savior be glory, majesty, power and authority, through Jesus Christ our Lord, before all ages, now and forevermore! Amen.

Reflection (5 minutes)

As a group, use the questions on page 94 to assess the effectiveness of your prayer time. Record any suggestions for improving the next session.

Encourage members to begin using the four kinds of responding prayers in their personal prayer times.

Session 4
Asking Prayers

Preparing to pray (5 minutes)
See "Preparing to Pray" for session 1 on page 86 Because of day 5's emphasis on praying in agreement with God and others, some may need to spend a few minutes with one another seeking forgiveness or reconciliation. Encourage them to do this.

Prayer Time (50 minutes)

1. *Confession.* Acknowledge God's presence and participation in your prayer time. Ask members to confess truths about God and their relationships with Him.

2. *Praise, Worship, and Thanksgiving.* These three kinds of prayer blend together well. Spend time responding to God's attributes, glory, and riches. Read or sing a thanksgiving hymn together.

3. *Petition.* Focus this time of petition on praying for your group and/or your church. You may want to pray for:
- Unity
- Perseverance
- Purity
- Generosity
- Wisdom
- Knowledge
- Faithfulness
- Peace
- Prayerfulness
- Love
- Understanding
- Boldness

4. *Intercession.* Now focus your praying on others. Allow members to pray requests for the concerns they have. Consider praying for some of the following as well:

- Broken, hurting persons in the news
- Single parents
- Persons in nursing homes
- Sick and homebound persons
- Missionaries overseas
- Missionaries at home
- War-torn areas of the world
- Refugees
- Christian ministries
- Prisoners (lost and Christian)
- Other churches
- The homeless, poor, and oppressed
- Orphans and widows
- Persons who are grieving

5. *Closure.* Lead the group in prayer.

Reflection (5 minutes)

As a group, use the questions on page 94 to assess the effectiveness of your prayer time. Record any suggestions for improving the next session.

Suggest that members learn during their personal prayer times to pray according to God's will by considering His viewpoint and by stating reasons for Him to respond to their requests.

Session 5
Petition

Preparing to Pray (5 minutes)

See "Preparing to Pray" for session 1 on page 87. Pay special attention this week to responding to others' prayers (see the suggestions on p. 72). Group members may need to pray for faith instead of unbelief, for right motives, and for forgiveness for sins that hinder intimacy with the Father.

Prayer Time (50 minutes)

1. *Confession.* Acknowledge God's presence and participation in your prayer time. Ask members to confess truths about God and their relationships with Him. Focus especially on truths about God as Father and their relationships with Him as children.

2. *Praise.* Praise your Heavenly Father by lifting up His qualities like patience, kindness, gentleness, tenderness, strength, protection, fairness, justice, mercy, peacefulness, faithfulness, forgiveness, slowness to anger, understanding, and wisdom. Exalt His love, which is unconditional, pure, everlasting, safe, and trustworthy.

3. *Worship.* Encourage members to express their love and adoration for their Heavenly Father. Ask each person to give one reason for loving the Father.

4. *Thanksgiving.* Ask members to express their gratitude to God for all He has done. They should think about all He has done as Heavenly Father for them, His children. Ask them to thank Him for adopting them into His family, for giving them His name, and for giving His only Son for their redemption. They should thank God for giving them an inheritance that is eternal. Encourage members to thank Him for every good and perfect gift; for His tough love, which will not let them stray far away without using loving discipline to call them back; and for His provision for their specific needs.

5. *Petition and Intercession.* Spend a greater portion of your prayer time focusing on petition. Encourage members to request prayer for personal needs or concerns. Rather than state a request to the group, participants may choose to pray for their own needs or concerns. As one prays for a personal concern, encourage the rest of the group to respond to the prayer and to join in intercession. Continue praying for one another in inter-

cession as long as the Holy Spirit guides you. You may find that the personal concerns lead you to intercession for related persons or concerns. Give the Holy Spirit great freedom to guide your praying during this session.

6. *Closure.* Join hands in a circle. Encourage volunteers to pray one-sentence prayers summarizing prayer burdens or expressing praise, worship, or thanksgiving to the Father.

Reflection (5 minutes)

As a group, use the questions on page 94 to assess the effectiveness of your prayer time. Record any suggestions for improving the next session.

Encourage members to use the principles in week 5 during their personal prayer times to make prayers of petition to the Lord.

Session 6

Intercession

Preparing to Pray (5 Minutes)

See "Preparing to Pray" for session 1 on page 87. Encourage group members to focus on who God is.

Prayer Time (45 minutes)

1. *Confession.* Acknowledge God's presence and participation in your prayer time. Ask members to confess truths about God and their relationships with Him. Allow time for members to confess their sins to one another and to pray for one another (see *Jas. 5:16*).

2. *Praise.* Lift up God's attributes in praise. Consider mentioning these: almighty, abounding in love, all-knowing, all-powerful, always present, eternal, faithful, flawless, forgiving, gentle, good, gracious, holy, jealous, just, majestic, merciful, patient, peaceful, perfect, pure, righteous, slow to anger, sure, true, understanding, and wise.

3. *Worship.* Ask members to express to the Lord their love, adoration, reverence, and honor. They should tell Him how much they need Him or long to be with Him.

4. *Thanksgiving.* Encourage members to count their blessings: spiritual, physical, and material. Thank God for the wonderful works He has done.

5. *Petition and Intercession.* Because day 5 directs members to focus on God's will for them, their group, and their church, take time to focus on prayer for God's purposes. Encourage members to share from pages 83-85 what they sense to be God's will and purposes for their church. Explain that this kind of sharing is a part of praying together. Members need to hear from one another and from the Lord through others. Listen to learn whether several members mention similar or identical concerns. These may indicate directions in which to focus your praying. Pray for God's purposes as He leads your praying.

Lead a time of petition by praying for yourself and your group, focusing on guidance, wisdom, spiritual growth, the filling of the Spirit, spiritual fruit, daily bread, God's provisions, deliverance from temptation, and protection.

Encourage members to intercede for the calling of Christian workers, Christian fruit, unity, bold witnessing, the filling of the Holy Spirit, deliverance, missionaries, reconciliation, right conduct, all saints, your enemies, love, knowledge, understanding, wisdom, preservation, persons in authority. Let God–your Master–guide your continued intercession for specific needs of others and for His work.

6. *Closure.* Summarize what you sense God has done during your prayer time. Thank Him for the privilege of praying together. Ask Him to make your church a house of prayer for the nations.

Reflection (10 minutes)

Discuss the value of this study and the prayer times you have had together. Allow members to share brief testimonies of what God has done in their lives during their daily study and during the group prayer times.

Discuss: What do you sense that God wants you to do next to continue the process of becoming a house of prayer? Consider these ideas:

1. Continue meeting monthly, weekly, or daily for concentrated periods of praying together.
2. Study *Experiencing God: Knowing and Doing the Will of God, Youth Edition* by Henry Blackaby and Claude King.
3. Study *When God Speaks, Youth Edition*, by Henry Blackaby and Richard Blackaby.
4. Study *The Notebook: A DiscipleYouth Experience*, Compiled by R. Clyde Hall, Jr. and Dean Finley.

5. Participate in the Youth Prayer Corp by contacting the Youth Section, 127 Ninth Avenue North, Nashville, TN 37234-0152 or call 615-251-2855.
6. Locate other prayer resources to guide the direction and subjects of your praying. Examples are:
   • A church prayer list
   • A prayer-ministry newsletter
   • A missions newsletter, magazine, or prayer-request list
   • A denominational prayer list or newspaper listing concerns for prayer

---

* Resources may be purchased from the Customer Service Center, 127 Ninth Avenue North, Nashville, TN 37234; 1-800-458-2772; or from a Baptist Book Store or a Lifeway Christian Store.

Suggestions for Praying Together

1. Acknowledge God's presence and active participation with you in prayer.

2. Use common language rather than church words.

3. Speak for yourself, using I, me, my, or mine rather than we, us, our, or ours.

4. Save all of your closings (like "Amen" and "In Jesus' name") until the end of the prayer period.

5. Prepare yourselves through prayers of confession, cleansing, and reconciliation.

6. Spend time in prayers of worship, praise, and thanksgiving.

7. Spend the bulk of your time in prayers of petition and intercession. Share requests as you pray rather than spend time at the beginning to list and discuss requests.

8. Pray about one subject at a time

9. Take turns praying about a subject. Continue on that subject as long as God seems to guide the praying.

10. Be specific in what you ask of God.

11. Ask the Holy Spirit to guide your praying according to God's will. Pay attention to the Holy Spirit's direction for praying.

12. Consider God's viewpoint and give God a reason to answer.

13. Use biblical principles, patterns, and promises to guide your requests.

14. Seek Spirit-guided agreement with others in your prayers.

15. Seek to put yourself in the place of those for whom you are praying so that you can "feel" what they feel.

16. Listen to the prayers of others for direction or answers to your prayers.

17. Respond to the prayers of others.

18. Pray for one another.

19. When time permits, pray until God is finished with you.

20. Consider writing down the subjects for which you have prayed so that you can watch with anticipation for God's answers.

21. When God answers one of your prayers, remember to thank Him and watch for opportunities to testify to His wonderful work.

Questions for Reflecting on Group Prayer Sessions

1. At particular times did you sense God's presence in a special way? When and how?

2. Did you spend most of your time in prayer rather than discuss prayer or share prayer requests?

3. Did you take time for confession, praise, worship, and thanksgiving? Was it meaningful or just ritual?

4. Did you pray about one subject at a time, or did individuals tend to pray through a list of several unrelated requests at one time?

5. Were your requests to God specific, or were they general and vague? Will you recognize when God answers your requests?

6. Did you use Bible promises, patterns, examples, or principles in your praying? Were they meaningful or helpful? Have any come to mind after your prayer session that would have been meaningful? If so, share them with the group.

7. Did you give God a reason to answer your prayer?

8. Did you come to a sense of Spirit-led agreement about the direction of your request? Did your faith increase?

9. Did you listen to and respond to others' prayers?

10. Did you pray for one another?

Kinds of Prayer

PRAYER	Nature of the Prayer
Confession	Responding to God's holiness
Praise	Responding to God's attributes
Worship	Responding to God's glory
Thanksgiving	Responding to God's riches
Petition	Asking that is led by Your Heavenly Father
Intercession	Asking that is led by Your Master

Christian Growth Study Plan

In the **Christian Growth Study Plan (formerly Church Study Course)**, this book *In God's Presence, Youth Edition* is a resource for course credit in the subject area Prayer of the Christian Growth category of diploma plans. To receive credit, read the book, complete the learning activities, show your work to your pastor, a staff member or church leader, then complete the following information.

Send the completed page to the Christian Growth Study Plan, 127 Ninth Avenue North, MSN 117, Nashville, TN 37234-0117. This page may be duplicated. FAX: (615) 251-5067.

For information about the Christian Growth Study Plan, refer to the current Christian Growth Study Plan Catalog. Your church office may have a copy. If not, request a free copy from the Christian Growth Study Plan office (615/251-2525).

In God's Presence, Youth Edition
CG-0249

PARTICIPANT INFORMATION

Social Security Number	Personal CGSP Number*	Date of Birth

Name (First, MI, Last)
☐ Mr. ☐ Miss
☐ Mrs. ☐

Home Phone

Address (Street, Route, or P.O. Box)

City, State

Zip Code

CHURCH INFORMATION

Church Name

Address (Street, Route, or P. O. Box)

City, State

Zip Code

CHANGE REQUEST ONLY

☐ Former Name

☐ Former Address

City, State

Zip Code

☐ Former Church

Zip Code

Signature of Pastor, Conference Leader, or Other Church Leader

Date

*New participants are requested but not required to give SS# and date of birth. Existing participants, please give CGSP# when using SS# for the first time. Thereafter, only one ID# is required.